SILENT
MIND
PUTTING

ALSO BY ROBIN SIEGER

BOOKS
Natural Born Winners
You Can Change Your Life Anytime You Want
42 Days to Wealth, Health and Happiness
Passport to Success
Silent Mind Golf
Golf's Moment of Truth

AUDIO
Natural Born Winners
Pathway to Peace of Mind
Pathway to Success
NBW Guided Meditation

SILENT MIND PUTTING

ROBIN SIEGER

First published in Great Britain
2013 by Aurum Press Ltd
74–77 White Lion Street,
London N1 9PF
www.aurumpress.co.uk

A catalogue record for this book is available from the British Library.

ISBN 978 1 78131 047 2

1 3 5 7 9 10 8 6 4 2
2014 2016 2017 2015 2013

Typeset by Saxon Graphics Ltd, Derby
Printed and bound in Great Britain by Clays Ltd, St Ives plc

To
Kersh, Large, Indiana, Falcy,
Dodge, Sharps, Gordy
and
All Past Members of the B Team Tour

CONTENTS

CONTENTS

PLAY

FOREWORD

People who are successful in life make things happen and at the same time make things simple. To get to that point they have to prepare well, learn from others, find out what works, work at it and then execute a plan. Robin, a keen golfer whose teaching on success has helped thousands of individuals improve their performance in their business and personal lives is now applying the same approach to the mystical art of putting. With his new book *Silent Mind Putting* Robin has done a great job in making golfers aware of the simplicity of putting and of how to become much better putters than they are now, by mastering the mental game.

It is an insightful book on an aspect of the game that has been studied exhaustively since golf's very beginnings: how to get that little white object into that 4¼ inch hole! When one is putting well, it certainly feels simple – the putts are easy to read, one senses the pace and the hole looks like a bucket. On the other hand when the putts keep missing, left and right, it is as if there is no hole on the green at all. How can that be? 'Change this', or 'Change that' is the popular doctrine. 'It's all luck and mine was all bad', 'The greens were poor', 'They were too slow', 'They were too fast', 'I had no feel' are amongst the many excuses offered up.

As many golfers who seek improvement have a plan for their long game, so equally must they have one for their putting. After all it is half of the game and the easiest area for most golfers to really improve upon and lower their scores. Not nearly enough importance is placed on putting even amongst some top players, believe it or not. Look at most practice areas at golf clubs and you will see the range is busy and the putting green empty. In my experience, if a player misses a few short putts during a round they put it down to 'one of those days', but when a golfer hits a couple of drives out of bounds, once the round is over they are soon off to the practice tee, booking a lesson, etcetera, etcetera. Unfortunately so much less emphasis is placed on the value of putting.

This book will open your eyes as to its importance, and what you can do to lessen your number of putts. By making it more of a priority and enjoying the process along the way, you will score better and have more fun – and that after all, is what the game is all about.

Enjoy the read,

David Leadbetter
Florida, USA
February 2013

INTRODUCTION

Putting is easy. Or at least it should be.

The putting stroke is not about power, or how far we can hit the ball. We don't need to shape the shot. There are no hazards, no out of bounds and no bad lies. It is the easiest golf shot imaginable, isn't it?

A great wealth of advice exists to help the average golfer become a better putter, but all the theories, approaches and techniques boil down to two fundamentals, agreed upon by almost all the teachers, analysts and experts:

1. You must have a stroke that brings the club head squarely back to the ball.
2. You need to strike the ball down the correct line of the putt.

Do these two things and the odds are that you will be a good putter. What could be simpler?

Take someone who has never played golf before – a complete non-golfer. Ask them to make a shot with a driver or an iron and you will be lucky if they make contact with the ball. The use of these clubs requires considerable skill. Yet almost anyone can pick up a putter and make a decent stroke on the ball. And within a few minutes of experimentation, a non-player can start enjoying the feel of making a putt.

So if the putt is a simple stroke on a technical level, how hard, actually, can putting be? Why do we need to work on our putting technique? Why are there so many books dedicated to exploring the mechanics of the putt, packed with suggestions to help us perfect our stroke and improve our success on the green? Why do we need to work on our mental approach to, seemingly, the simplest aspect of the game?

The reality, for most of us, is that the putting green is the place where most shots are dropped. It is a peculiar fact of golf that there are more demons to be found lurking on this smooth grassy carpet than on any other part of the course. So it should be no surprise that by improving their putting the average golfer can save more strokes per round more quickly than in any other part of their game.

For most of us this is not reflected in our practice routine. Proportionally, we spend a lot more time practising the longer shots than we do the game played on the green. We go to the driving range and work our way through our clubs but stop when we reach the putter. Just before we go out on the course we may spend a few minutes on the practice green. In our mind we are thinking, 'I better find out what the pace of the greens is today,' but we could hardly call this serious practice. Perhaps the very simplicity of putting has deceived us?

The demons of the green are not reserved for us amateurs. Many of the game's greatest players retired when they could no longer sink their putts. From tee to green their game was as good as ever, but the green became a place of nightmares.

Legends of the game have been assailed by uncertainty, self-doubt and mental paralysis on the green. In his final years as a pro, Ben Hogan would freeze over the ball when putting. He was almost unable to draw the club back. Sam Snead tried hundreds of different putters. He finally adopted a side-saddle method that was later banned by the golfing authorities. It seems ironic that the easiest and most instinctive stroke in the game has been the downfall of many of golf's greats.

Putting has been called a game within a game. Most golf shots are played in the air; all putts are played over the ground. It has more subtle variables and moments of high drama. The final putt in every major is introduced by the commentator in reverential, hushed tones as, 'This for the championship.' And of course, if that putt drops it ensures the player's place in history and guarantees huge financial reward. It makes a whole new challenge of that seemingly simple shot.

Consider the pressure that Ernie Els and Adam Scott were under as they putted on the eighteenth green in the 2012 Open at Royal Lytham & St Anne's. Els knew he had to sink his putt to put himself into any kind of contention. Scott knew he had to hole his to get into a play-off. How they felt over those putts we humble amateurs can only imagine, but we can understand the degree to which the technical difficulty of the putts as pure golfing shots was outweighed by the pressure of the situation.

We may never experience the same pressure as the pro golfer. But in our own game, at whatever level, we experience our own high-pressure situations, and we can develop our own confidence, instinct and touch to improve our results. How do we do this?

There are players who seem to have the ability to nail putt after putt from just about anywhere on the green. When we watch tournaments on television, we hear experts comment on the different putting abilities of players – who is poor and who is good. So surely all we have to do is watch the good putters, identify what they're doing right and copy it, and our own putting will improve?

We all know that isn't enough. Because we also need to understand how they manage their mental game on the green: how they read their putt, how they put the right amount of power into their stroke, and how they manage to get themselves into the right state of mental control so that they do not change their rhythm or tempo when under pressure.

When I speak to professional golfers they tell me that golf is 80 per cent mental and 20 per cent mechanical, but I would argue that on the putting surface the mental aspect of the game increases, so that putting becomes 90 per cent mental. Our earlier experiment with a non-golfer who quickly masters the putting stroke supports this theory. The same level of mechanical competence with a lob wedge and a dozen balls would take considerable time to develop. So why does the mental side of our putting game hold such power over us? I have spoken to many players over the years, and I have learned this:

Good putters expect to putt well and make putts. Poor putters *hope* to putt well but don't really *believe* they will make many.

I have played with outstanding golfers who use antique equipment and very unorthodox styles. But game after game they break the hearts of their opponents by sinking putts which appear to defy the law of averages. I know one well-known former Scotland rugby player who still plays with the putter he used when he was a boy. He has to bend almost double to use the club – but it works for him.

When I speak to these players about their putting they are confident enough to describe themselves as good putters. This confidence is so important because golf is not only a game of style and technique, it is also a game of self-mastery. And nowhere is that more important than on the putting green.

How can we free ourselves from the inevitable pressures of putting? How can we create self-belief, and expect to make our putts, rather than just hoping that we will? How can we remove the self-doubt which creeps into our minds as we take our stance on the green and prepare to putt for the match?

Much of my working life has been spent teaching people about peak performance and success. I have spoken to business leaders, companies, sportsmen and -women and many others about how to remove self-doubt and prepare mentally for the challenges we face – in business, in sport and in life. I have lectured to some of the biggest companies in the world, and have written a number of books, including the international bestseller *Natural Born Winners*, which explores the mental aspects of success in great detail. I have made success my speciality, if you like, and have learnt a great deal from the many people I have met along the way.

However, I realised a number of years ago that I had not translated these theories of peak performance into the reality of success on the golf course. Despite playing golf for twenty-five years, and being a decent player back in college, I was a poor golfer with a handicap I wasn't proud of. One day on the course a friend gently enquired: if I was this supposed expert on success, peak performance and the mind, why was I such a terrible golfer?

Some years earlier I had realised that the things I did in life without thinking were done easily and automatically, free from self-doubt, anxiety or concern. But out on the course, in my pursuit of golfing excellence, I was thinking too much, worrying about mis-hitting the shot in hand and, like many golfers, being unnecessarily harsh on myself. I realised I needed to turn my thinking about peak performance onto my own game: 'Physician, heal thyself!'

I spent a long time thinking over my conundrum, and eventually had an insight. I didn't jump out of the bath shouting, 'Eureka!', but I did begin to see where the problem lay: my thoughts were impeding my performance. I resolved to stop thinking over the shot and instead play instinctively, free from concerns about anything other than the stroke in hand. In simple terms, I finally managed to get out of my own way. Three rounds of golf later my handicap had dropped from sixteen to eight.

Having seen such a dramatic improvement, I continued to explore the mental game change I had experienced in greater depth. I developed a mental approach to playing golf which I came to call the **silent mind**. My book about this approach, *Silent Mind Golf*, explains how golfers can master their thoughts and their emotions when they are on the course if they incorporate the mental side of the game in their practice, through mental conditioning and relaxation techniques. The book's success, and the testimonials I receive, leave me in no doubt that the mind remains the most overlooked aspect of the game. Conversely, when properly and methodically addressed, the mental side of golf provides the single greatest – and most immediate – opportunity for improvement.

Having learnt how to silence the mind and 'get out of my own way', I turned my attention, in my next book, *Golf's Moment of Truth*, to the thorny issue of choking, again examining the psychological hurdles that can disrupt our ability to play the shot we want to play, and suggesting ways in which we can overcome the mental and emotional distractions that arise while we're out on the course.

Now I have chosen to focus right in on a single aspect of the game and address the key moment on any hole: the shot which completes the process, the point of closure and the stroke where the potential for mental interference is highest – the putt. As we have discussed, the putt should be the simplest of shots, yet its context makes it highly-pressured, and the area where most golfers drop shots. What better place to employ the silent mind techniques than the part of our game that can make the biggest difference to our score?

This book is an exploration of the mental game of putting. It is a combination of reflections, tips, exercises and suggestions. There is no magnificent secret to be revealed, but there are insights and lessons that I believe will help us become the best putters we can be. There are changes we can make to our mental and attitudinal approach to putting which will help us master our minds when under pressure to close out a hole.

Before we move on to examine the world of putting in more detail, let's look briefly at what the silent mind approach entails.

WHAT IS THE SILENT MIND?

Silent mind golf is not a system, philosophy or quick-fix method. Rather it is a simple process to develop the critical mental skills needed to perform at a level of unconscious excellence unimpeded by thought.

For a game that is more mental than mechanical, mastery over the mind becomes an essential skill. Yet very few players do any real structured mental conditioning work, beyond having a vague grasp of staying positive and relaxed, and breathing deeply when feeling stressed. This is not enough. If we cannot master our emotions off the course, we should not expect to control them on the course.

The silent mind approach shows the golfer how to develop the mental skills and strengths required during competition and emphasises the importance of making them a regular part of the practice regime. The process involves three simple steps:

Focus. On every shot, from the opening tee shot to the three-inch tap-in on the final green, we must focus our attention on the place we want the ball to finish. This is the spot that becomes the target, and that target needs to be in our mind's eye. Just as the archer focuses on the bullseye, and not the arrow, and the race driver focuses on the road ahead, and not the steering wheel, so too as golfers we need always to have a target upon which we focus our mind before we hit the shot. The target is not the ball; it is the final resting place of the shot. How often do golfers focus on where they do *not* want the ball to go, then announce in a comically astonished manner, 'I can't believe I did that!'?

Faith is the second aspect of playing more instinctively. When we have confidence in our ability to do something successfully we relax. We do it naturally and instinctively. When driving a car, we do so in a state of confidence, trusting in our ability, despite the potential dangers. Far too often on the golf course players entertain self-doubt: 'I hope I hit the fairway . . . Don't knock it in the water . . .' If we don't believe we can make a shot, it is an odds-on certainty we won't. *Faith is simply trusting in ourselves*: if we have faith in our ability to play a shot, we will be more inclined to relax and perform intuitively and instinctively. But that faith must be grounded in experience and not wishful thinking.

The final aspect of the silent mind approach is the one I always knew people would understand but find hardest to apply. This aspect is **Presence**. In its simplest form it means to 'be in the present moment', or, as I have heard it expressed very succinctly, to 'be here now'. Too often our anxieties on the course are about poor shots we have played earlier on, or poor shots we imagine await us later in the round. If we shut out all thoughts about the past or the future, and any feelings associated with those thoughts, then we are in the moment, and free from emotional input. We have a silent mind – which is the perfect state to be in when we are playing a shot.

In the coming pages we will discover how the silent mind approach applies especially on the putting green. We will develop new themes along the same lines, and work through a specific set of principles and mental drills that will enable us to putt with confidence.

Just as every good story needs a beginning, middle and end, and a narrative thread that connects them, I also believe learning and mastery require structure. I have divided this book according to three distinct perspectives – Prepare, Perceive and Play – which help to build our understanding and provide a logical approach to improvement. And as the book gives us an insight into our own mental game, it is my desire that it will help us approach the putting green with confidence, not just hoping to sink that putt but *expecting* to do so, and that, as a result, we will find ourselves putting like champions.

Robin Sieger
Sarasota, USA
January 2013

PREPARE

1

PREPARE

'Before anything else, preparation is the key to success.'

Alexander Graham Bell

In golf, as in life, it is essential to be as prepared as possible for the task ahead. While this applies to all aspects of the game, it is particularly true on the putting green. **If we want to produce our very best, we need to be prepared long before we reach the first green.**

Surely all I am doing is stating the obvious? In my experience, most golfers think putting is the simplest of the strokes, so they make the assumption that they *are* prepared. But the fact is that they are not. They may be ready to play the game, they may be ready to walk onto the putting surface, but they are not mentally prepared in a way which gives them the optimal chance to do their best.

To illustrate this point, I want you to compare putting to other seemingly simple activities. Let me give you some very practical non-sporting examples:

Let's start with painting a room. I am sure we all think painting a room is a pretty straightforward task. We need some paint and a brush. Maybe a ladder. We'll put down some dust sheets to catch any drips. We'll give the surface a quick rub down and then paint away. Once we are finished, we'll stand back and admire the job. The room will have been painted. Job done! But we all know there are other criteria. Has the job been done well? Does it show signs of inexperience or haste on the part of the painter? Will it last?

Think back to the last time you asked a professional painter and decorator to do a job in your house. For him, the most important part of the job is the preparation. He thoroughly prepares all the surfaces, which takes much longer than we expect. He fills in any small holes on the walls or the woodwork with the appropriate filler. He sands the surfaces down until they are perfectly level and smooth. Once he is happy with the surfaces he has prepared, he finds the right type of paint for the job. He uses good quality brushes, not a packet of brushes from a discount store. The professional painter knows that the secret to a good job is in the preparation. The more he works on the surfaces he is going to paint, the easier his job is. When he is finished you can see the difference. It is a job that will last. You can tell it has not been done with poor quality brushes, a few tins of cheap paint and a slap-dash attitude.

The same applies to cooking. A professional chef will tell you that the art of cooking has its foundations in preparation. If you have watched cooking shows on television, or seen professional chefs in a working kitchen, you cannot fail to be impressed by the amount of preparation which goes on before any food is actually cooked. Without the right ingredients, sourced and properly prepared, the dish can never be perfect. And no amount of improvisation will ever hide that fact.

In exactly the same way, we would expect a surgeon who is about to undertake a major operation to prepare thoroughly for the task ahead. She has studied the case in detail, and is familiar with the patient's medical history. She knows the procedures she will employ, and the implements she requires to execute them. She knows what to do if the operation does not go to plan long before she makes the first incision. She is prepared.

We need to take the same commitment to preparation onto the putting green. Naturally, we want to be the best putters we can be. That doesn't happen by wishing or imagining. Every golfer needs to work on their skills. Even the most gifted players have worked hard to improve the way they play. Show me a winner and I will show you someone who prepared to win. Show me a world-class performer and I will show you someone who prepared for success through practice, analysis and dedication. Think of the gold medallists at the London Olympics: their success didn't just happen on the day; it took years of dedication and preparation for each one of them to reach that podium. It took preparation.

The question we need to ask is: **How good a putter could I be if I dedicated time and practice to improving my game?** What could I achieve if I understood and applied proper preparation to my putting in the way that I work on other aspects of my game?

Most animals are creatures of habit. If you have a pet, a dog or a cat, you will know from experience that its behaviour from day to day is absolutely predictable. We human beings like to think we are a cut above the animals, but we are also fairly predictable in the way we behave. We generally like to eat the same food in the same restaurants. We buy the same style of trousers. We go back to the same places on holiday. We have our favourite chair at home. And on the golf course we follow the same patterns of thinking and playing. We have habits and superstitions which we repeat every time we arrive at the course.

I want you to stop reading for a moment and think about the routine you follow when you arrive at your golf club. From driving into the car park to walking onto the first tee, I bet that you follow the same routine every time you play.

These routines are unconscious. They become automatic. In fact their repetition makes us feel comfortable. Rarely, if ever, do we stop to question if they are beneficial.

Now think about the routine you follow when you putt. What habits do you repeat each time you walk onto the green? Most of us take a few practice strokes with the putter, read the line and swing the club. And hope that we sink the putt. In our minds we know it has worked well enough on many occasions in the past, and when it hasn't – well that's golf, isn't it? So we follow the same approach and hope for the best.

If there is an overlooked area of putting, it is the mental and mechanical preparation that takes place before we take the putter out of the bag. We need to prepare ourselves for what we are about to do. From the moment we take the putter from our bag we must be mentally and mechanically free from any stress or worry, and this mental state should continue until we return the club to the bag. Then we can allow our mind to wander again. I believe such a mental approach can be the most significant addition to the amateur golfer's putting armoury.

In order to be the best putter we can be we must have a stroke we trust, a club we love and feel comfortable with, a pre-shot routine that never varies, the capacity to trust our instinct to read the line, the skill to apply the right amount of pace and a relaxed mind which is totally unconscious with regard to the execution of the stroke.

Do we really need to put so much emphasis on preparation? Aren't we over-complicating the putt with too much analysis? We have all watched the great golfers on television who seem to step up and just hit the ball. There doesn't seem to be too much fuss or science there.

Of course, what we are seeing with those great putters is the *result* of good preparation, not the beginning of the process. What seems to be a casual stroke has taken years of hard work to perfect.

We can all learn from the top performers, not only golfers but people from the worlds of business and other sports as well. **The key characteristics of all top performers are confidence and a supreme will to win.** If we consider successful people in sport and business, whether it is Tiger Woods, Warren Buffet or Michael Phelps, one thing is clear. They not only have an overwhelming desire to succeed, they have an absolute conviction of their ability to do so. They have a confidence which is grounded in a powerful self-belief, in turn created through positive reinforcement from their family, their peers and themselves and, perhaps most importantly, as a consequence of repeated practice. Every success thereafter is a further re-enforcement of the positive self-image they have of themselves as winners.

Jack Nicklaus has said that the most difficult major to win was his first. After he had won his first he felt that every time he played in a major he could win it. He had instilled in himself that confidence and self-belief that he was a winner and he took that onto the golf course with him every time.

Success breeds success, just as failure breeds more failure. How often do we stand over a putt and find our brain supplying reasons why the putt won't go in the hole? Even before we've struck the ball!

We need to **adopt a winning attitude when we go onto the golf course, believing we will win**. We need to be positive about our game and particularly our putting. We need to think about how good a putter we can be. The putting green is where we can most quickly save strokes and reduce our handicap. What a difference it would make to our scores if we could cut the total number of putts by only two or three per round.

Preparation is as critical to success as its absence is to failure. We cannot simply hope that our putting is on form all the time. We need to prepare a strategy for putting success. Naturally, a large part of this strategy will be practice. I don't know many people who truly enjoy practice, 'It's boring!' being the most frequent complaint. But the key to successful practice is to make it purposeful.

A friend of mine served in the British Army for over 19 years, most of them in an elite unit. He told me that they trained and trained and trained. It was repetitive and endless, but never without real purpose. He used two expressions which illustrate the value of purposeful practice: the first was, 'Train hard, fight easy,' and the second was, 'Remember the seven Ps: **proper planning and preparation prevent pretty poor performance**.'

Walking onto the green is not the same as going to war, but these same lessons are valuable and applicable nonetheless.

1. **Practise with purpose; practise as you mean to play**. Give your full attention to practice, so that when it's for real, it will feel familiar and less stressful.
2. Plan and prepare your training. **Don't hit balls for the sake of it; always engage your imagination and mind.**
3. **Luck has nothing to do with long-term success.**

One aid to proper putting preparation is to get a putting journal, and to record our putting practice: the drills followed, the number of putts taken, the number of putts made, and of course the number of putts taken per round played.

Proper preparation and planning can take us from the putters we are today to becoming the best putters we can be. I believe we can go from being mediocre to being magnificent. And we can walk onto every green with a strong positive feeling. If we are prepared.

2

DON'T DESPAIR!

'Bad putting is due more to the effect the green has upon *the player* than the effect it has upon *the action of the ball*.'

Bobby Jones

Despair on the putting green is the most unsettling of emotions. It saps our energy, dominates our thoughts and makes us miserable. It takes any joy out of our experience. I have met many golfers who simply despair of their putting. Their game is solid enough from tee to green, but then the troubles start. 'If only I could putt,' they say with a gloomy shrug of the shoulders and the despair of an unjustly condemned man.

Reaching a point of despair on the greens is a gradual process, a slow accumulation of self-doubt and poor putting over a period of time. It is rarely the result of one missed putt or one bad round. Despair does not allow us to appreciate the positive aspects of our putting. It causes us to dwell on our imperfections and feelings of inadequacy, and to search for a change which will improve things. The player generally swaps putters, changes routine and putting style, in a forlorn attempt to recover whatever they believe they have lost.

I have a friend who, in a few years, went from being a two-handicap golfer with a wonderful touch on the greens to a fifteen-handicapper with no feel or touch at all. It was truly painful to watch him putt.

Twelve-inch putts got jabbed two feet past the hole; four-putts were no longer the stuff of other people's horror stories. They had become his reality.

I had long conversations with him about this, and he confessed he could no longer draw the club back. He had no sense of pace on any putt at all. This may sound strange, but to those familiar with his experience, I am sure it makes perfect sense.

In his gloomier moments my friend talked about giving up the game. He could see no way that he was going to get better. Total despair! I gave him the same advice I would give anyone: accept the awful putting as a stage you are going through, stop over-analysing your technique, accept outcomes without judging yourself as being good or bad, and believe without any doubt that you will see an improvement. Six months later he had returned to his earlier good form. He stopped searching for something he thought he had lost and began trusting in what he had. As the feelings of despair subsided his confidence grew, his touch returned and he began to play more instinctively. **Failure to improve is never final unless we accept it as being so.**

Willie Park Sr was a Scottish golf professional in the very early days of the game. He was one of golf's pioneers. Born in 1833, Park began his working life as a caddy and, like so many of his fellow golfers, he was self-taught. He was one of the outstanding players of his generation. He won the Open Championship four times between 1860 and 1875, a long time to stay at the top of the game.

For all his professional success, Park is best remembered by golf historians for his putting. He played the game when the equipment was much less sophisticated, and used a ball known as a feathery. This was a ball made of pieces of leather stitched together, filled with bird feathers, hammered into a round shape and then coated with paint. The balls were hand-made, and no two balls were exactly alike. In

Park's day he did not play on the lightning fast, manicured greens of today's golf courses. He played on greens which were more akin to mown lawns. And yet he was the greatest putter of his age.

When Park died in 1903, his obituary in *Golf Illustrated* said of his putting: 'Here he was not merely good, not merely excellent, but brilliant . . . so deadly was he when he was within three or four yards of the hole.' From under twelve feet Park was considered to be deadly accurate and someone who did not miss.

Park delivered the now legendary quotation and insightful truth about putting when he said, 'A man who can putt is a match for anyone.' This was from a golfer who played the game 150 years ago. Using the basic equipment of his day he still appreciated that the player who can putt will win matches and tournaments. Park's analysis of putting is still true today.

How many of us are happy with our putting? As I talk to golfers of different abilities I find that few putt to any degree of personal satisfaction. This leads to disappointment, which can in turn lead to despair. The despairing golfer begins to believe that they can never get better. This belief is not a fact, but as long as they hold it to be true, it will sabotage their ability to improve.

There is an old saying: 'I will believe it when I see it.' When it comes to transforming our game and escaping frustration and even despair, the opposite is true: 'When we believe it, we'll see it.' This may sound like a New Age sound bite, but belief before behaviour is a significant principle of performance development. Think of an

Olympic gold medallist, a first-time major winner, a teenager learning to drive or a chef cooking a new dish. Before any of these achievements are realised, there needs to be a belief that it can be done.

Putting is the part of the game most influenced by our confidence and self-belief. If I were to watch a match between a player with a solid putting stroke but low confidence and a confident player with a poor technical ability, I would bet on the confident player to triumph. **We must drop any negative thoughts we have about ourselves as a putter.** Such thoughts become barriers to improvement. They will keep us locked into a cycle of low expectation, which will soon manifest itself on the green as poor putting. On the other hand, the confident player will continue to putt with a confident expectation, in spite of any technical imperfections.

We looked earlier at our unconscious routines. **If we think of ourselves as poor putters, this will become a belief, an unconscious and repeated behaviour**. It doesn't need to be so. Any habit we have learned, we can unlearn. We can become more aware of the way we think and the language we use in our inner monologue out on the course. Let's **pay no attention to negative thoughts;** let's simply banish them from our minds. **As we stand over a putt, we must be positive.** In our mind we should visualise the ball following the line we have chosen and hear the sound of the ball hitting the tin.

This sounds simple – because it is! **Form follows function. As we think, so we perform.** If we think positively, we are likely to perform positively. I am not suggesting that simply adopting this positive attitude to putting will see us sink every five-foot putt we undertake, but I can guarantee that this major attitudinal change will begin to work immediately and that we will see improvement. **If we are willing to invest the time to master the mental game on the green, we will become better putters.**

The average amateur golfer does not invest the time necessary to become a better putter. This is the harsh reality for so many of us. I have spoken to many golfers in an attempt to understand why this is so. Here is a selection of the main reasons people give for spending so little time on their putting skills:

I'm too busy to practise. Most golfers have busy work and home schedules. Spending an hour or two a week on practising their putting is unrealistic. This means we must address our priorities. We are only too busy if becoming a better putter doesn't matter. If it really matters, we will find the time. How much time do we spend watching television, drinking beer or cocktails, or simply doing nothing? We have to redefine 'busy'. This is not being 'too busy'. This is being too comfortable to do anything about it! Let's reassess our priorities and make the changes we need to make. Do any of the following excuses sound familiar?

1. *I've tried everything, but nothing works for me*. This excuse makes me want to get my handkerchief out for the 'pity party' about to begin. It reminds me of the overweight person who says they've tried every diet known to man but they can't lose weight. We know that is not true. What is true is that nothing will work unless we believe it is going to work. We must commit to making the change we want to realise – then take action!

2. *I've always been a poor putter.* I hear this one from people who think that putting is an aspect of the game you either have a gift for or don't. It's like someone who says they can't play the piano

because they've never been musical. The skills we require to putt well are not wholly instinctive. At the very beginning of this book I described how people who had never picked up a putter before could quite rapidly, without instruction, begin to make a workable putting stroke. There is a lot we can do to develop mechanical skills. To label ourselves a poor player incapable of change, simply because that's the way we've always been, quickly becomes a self-fulfilling prophesy.

3. *I have tried so many different putters; I can't find one that's right for me.* 'A bad workman always blames his tools' may be an old cliché, but like most clichés it holds a kernel of truth. I have seen too many people putt well with poor rental clubs over the years to believe that, technically, the putter makes such a huge difference. If you can't find *any* putter you are comfortable with, it's not the club that needs fixing!

Any golfer improves their chances of making more putts if they **see practice as an opportunity and not a chore**. We need to create a series of practice drills to address specific issues we may have on the green. Colin Montgomerie was always concerned about his close putting. He was never comfortable with putts below about three or four feet, so he developed a routine at the end of his practice session where he would sink 200 putts from this critical length. He would count to 200 and if he missed one he would go back to the beginning. When was the last time we practised 200 three-footers?

One of the most important questions to ask ourselves is why we play golf in the first place. I would suggest it is because we enjoy it. We enjoy the game, the camaraderie, the skill, the competition and the satisfaction we get when it goes right. If we become involved in a cycle of behaviour which emphasises a negative aspect of our game, specifically our putting, this will destroy not only our confidence but also our enjoyment of the game, and our performance on the course.

Despite my irreverence about the excuses players use to explain why they can't putt, I do empathise with the suffering brought about by loss of confidence. It must be dreadful to walk on to a putting green with the expectation that you can three-putt or worse from just about anywhere. I have spoken to former professional golfers who became anxious every time they walked onto the green. In their minds they had no idea how they were going to putt. They had lost their sense of touch and feel. They experimented with their stroke; they changed their putters frequently. They no longer felt they were in control. They knew their days on tour were numbered, and some even gave the game up for ever.

Ben Hogan is still regarded as one of the greatest golfers of all time. Hogan stopped winning when he developed the 'yips'. 'Yips' is a wonderful word but a horrible concept. The yips is a stroke-inhibiting action which becomes seemingly impossible to fix. It may consist of twitches, staggers, jerks or even simply an inability to bring the putter head back to the ball. From tee to green Hogan was as good at 50 as he had been at 30. But he could no longer putt. His confidence was gone. He had once been one of the most reliable putters from eight feet and under.

Hogan's most glorious year was 1953. He was forty-one. He won three majors – but little did he know that he would never win another. His putting began to let him down. On two subsequent occasions he reached the 72nd hole of the US Open needing two putts to reach a play-off, in which he knew he would be very tough to beat. On both occasions he three-putted. He knew his putting had become suspect, and it bothered him. He actually campaigned to reduce the importance of putting by lobbying to have the size of the golf cup increased! He argued that the game would be improved by rewarding the better ball-strikers who hit the green in regulation. His proposal never got much support.

Hogan never came to terms with his yips. His competitive career was over. He received thousands of letters from fans around the world with suggestions of how he could cure the problem. Legend has it he read every one of them, but never found the cure! Hogan's putting demise is an example of despair at its worst. The player loses hope.

Medical experts who have studied survivors of hazardous situations say that, without exception, it is those who keep hope alive who have the greatest chance of survival. In those who give up, hope dies. In terms of improving our putting game we must never lose hope.

There are examples of players who refused to give up hope, who persevered and conquered their fears of putting to continue their illustrious careers. The most notable is Bernhard Langer, the German professional and two-times Masters winner. Langer was amongst the best ball-strikers of all time, but more than once he lost his putting stroke completely. He had the yips but never gave up on finding strategies to overcome it. Langer is an example that we can all follow. We may never experience the pressure of golf at that level, but we all face our own challenges. **The reality is we can always get better**.

Failure to improve is only final if we accept it to be so. This happens when we give up believing in our ability to transform our game. We are responsible for our own ability to become a better putter. Our teaching professional can give us all the information and advice we require to become technically better, but it is up to us to turn theory into practice. If we genuinely believe we can improve, we have taken the first critical step in transforming our potential on the green.

3

LOVE YOUR PUTTER

**'It's a marriage. If I had to choose between
my wife and my putter, well, I'd miss her.'**

Gary Player

We all have a favourite club. It might be the club that feels most comfortable, or one that brings good memories. I'd wager that whatever club it is, it comes with a positive expectation that it will be struck well. It brings more confidence.

Our favourite club may even change through the year. With the woods we have a choice: if we're having a bad day on the tee box, we can rest the driver and use a three- or five-wood instead. When it comes to the irons we have even more choice: we can vary the iron, try a utility club, or manufacture different shots with clubs we feel comfortable with.

The putter is different. We carry only one. Once we embark on a round of golf with our putter, we have no choice, and we can be certain we'll need it on every hole we play. We have to use it – so we'd better love it and trust it.

Next time you watch a tournament on television observe how, once a player has hit his ball onto the green, the caddy immediately hands the player their putter. The putter is the club that spends the most time in a player's hands during a round of golf. There is logic to this. **The more time we spend with a club in our hands the more**

familiar and comfortable we become with it. This comfort is important. It reduces the likelihood of stress being induced by the club. We should always feel comfortable with our clubs. They should 'fit like a glove'. And this should be true of the putter more than any other club.

I want you to imagine a situation that is familiar to every golfer. You go into a golf superstore. Every major club manufacturer is represented. Every club you can think of is available. There are state-of-the-art bays where you can try out clubs and have your swing analysed. There is a full-sized putting green with a mind-boggling selection of putters to try out. You feel like the proverbial kid in the candy store, wandering around looking at the sheer variety of clubs on offer.

How do you choose? Which putter is the best one for you? Like everyone else, I tend to start by trying out the most expensive models: it stands to reason that the most expensive must be the best! I also like to try the popular brands which I know some of my favourite players use. Then there will be the clubs at the wackier end of the scale: clubs which guarantee to save you shots or cure some golfing ill. My personal favourites are the gimmicky looking putters, some of which would not be out of place in a modern art gallery.

Then suddenly, when I least expect it, I find it: the putter I like the look of. It feels balanced and comfortable in my hands. None of the marketing displays, the prices, manufacturers' logos or innovative construction techniques mean anything now, because this club just feels right as I stand over the ball. I try it on the putting green. The putts begin to sink. Sold! Love at first sight.

Perhaps I am being a bit romantic here, but the point is that **we need to find the putter that is best for us**. Like me, you have probably tried many putters. There may be a particular style of putter you prefer. My preference is for a putter with a flat blade and a goose neck offset at the club head. I recently decided I needed a new putter, so I made a number of trips to my local golf store and tried putter after putter in their putting bay. I could not make up my mind. But after four visits, some thorough testing and copious note-making, I had narrowed my choice to two putters. They were almost identical: the length, loft and lie were the same. Both weighed the same, looked the same, and felt right in my hand. My choice then became personal. I decided I preferred the one with the natural metal colour, and bought two: one lives in Florida with my American clubs and the other lives in Scotland.

Famously, BB King slept with his guitar, Lucille, under his pillow at night. This may be a step too far, but there does have to be a relationship between the golfer and his putter. Ben Crenshaw is reckoned to be one of the best putters ever. Crenshaw's relationship with his putter is so personal he has a name for it: Little Ben. The significance is clear: the putter is an extension of himself.

Putting is a mental game. Dave Stockton, the putting guru, and one of the all-time best putters on the US tour, said that he believed putting was 95 per cent mental. **How we feel about our putter is crucially important**. If we hate our putter or are just indifferent to it, we should change it. We need to **find a putter we love**. We want a club that works for us on every level. It should feel good and give us confidence. And if your wife objects to it being under your pillow at night, explain to her how precious it actually is!

Many men fantasise about cars. They talk about what car they will drive after they have won the lottery. They know the brand and model; they know the full performance specification, acceleration, top speed, torque and horse power. We must apply the same thinking to our dream putter: we must have the same passion for our putter that we would have for a dream car. It is the club we will use more than any other in our bag.

Take your time when you are replacing your putter. Go to a pro shop or golf store and spend time trying different putters over as many visits as you think you need. Speak to the staff; ask questions. Allow yourself to make an informed, rational choice. Don't make a sudden decision on a putter just because you hole four putts in a row in the store. Remember, this needs to be a club you want to live with.

When I was a boy I was given a very old putter with a hickory shaft. The club had been made in the 1920s. It had the manufacturer's name engraved on the back. It was the second club I had ever been given. I was five. I knew nothing about putters but it looked perfect to me. I used it for seven years until I decided I wanted a modern putter like those my golfing heroes played with. I moved on to a very simply designed putter called the Bullscye by Titleist. The Bullseye was designed by John Reuter Jr in the 1940s, and its design has not changed much since. I liked the look of it because it reminded me of the simple bladed putter I began with. Over the years I experimented with other putters, but it was a long time before I felt as fully confident about any of them as I had in those early days with the Bullseye.

Confidence is the bedrock of our ability to putt well. Playing with a putter we trust is an important part of building that confidence.

I have played golf with players who have the latest state-of-the-art drivers and irons, but who have 40-year old putters, with warped shafts and, in one case, no grip and a very aged, weary club head. Yet their owners had great confidence in them and affection for them, and wouldn't change them for anything. Most importantly of all, they did their job admirably.

Finding a putter we love is vital to improving our game. It will build confidence and enable us to putt well.

4

ALL IN THE HEAD

'A leading difficulty with the average player is that he totally misunderstands what is meant by concentration. He may think he is concentrating when he is merely worrying.'

Bobby Jones

My father was a family doctor in Glasgow. Impressively, while working five-and-a-half days a week, he also managed for a period to play off scratch. For as long as I knew him I can only ever remember him using one putter. In fact he used the same putter for most of his life. It was an upright putter with a small face that was half the height of the ball. It was very light and had a thin, square leather grip. I bet when he bought it, *it* was considered a modern putter. Today I imagine it is an object of historical curiosity, worthy of inclusion in a museum. His putting style was as individual as the putter. He hunched over the ball, hands close to his chest, his head slightly turned to the left. He initiated the stroke with a very pronounced forward press. He used the same stroke on every putt. The only difference was the length of his backswing and follow-through.

I have never forgotten a story that he told me. When he was a young medical student he attended a lecture about parasites that live on the human body. The subject was body lice, or, to give them their correct name, *Pediculus humanus corporis.* In the interests of science the lecturer had arranged for some samples to be exhibited under a microscope. He invited the students to come and have a look through the lens, one at a time. My father said when he looked into the lens there were all these tiny little monsters which live on the body and feed on blood and dead skin. The little blighters then laid and glued clusters of eggs onto hair follicles. It was not a pretty sight! The lecturer then started to scratch himself, as if some of the lice had escaped and attached themselves to him. It was infectious. Before too long a number of the students were beginning to scratch as well. They believed they were infested with a louse or two. The lecturer then stopped and announced there was no chance that anyone had been infested; his scratching was simply to demonstrate the power of imagination and auto-suggestion. That lesson changed the way my father listened to and examined his patients – and the way he played golf too.

My father's medical practice was in a blue-collar part of Glasgow. He saw hundreds of patients every month. There were many with genuine illnesses in need of medical and surgical intervention, but he said there were far more patients for whom, in his words, it was 'all in their head'.

We underestimate the power of our thoughts and imagination. The influence our thinking will have on our game is much greater than we realise. Henry Ford famously said, 'If you think you can or think you can't, you're usually right.' I have always believed that this applies to the putting green. If we stand over a putt and think we'll make it, we give ourselves the best opportunity to do so. If we are thinking we'll miss it, we probably will.

Much of our success is due to belief and attitude. Ask yourself, what kind of putter do you believe you are? Are you a good putter, or a poor putter? The golfer who has been infected with the belief that he is a bad putter will begin to lose confidence and subsequently the touch and feel for the putting stroke. **What we believe about our ability to putt will influence our future perceptions and expectations of our putting**.

Perception is what we observe and sense on the green. Do we see challenges and degrees of difficulty, with possible disaster only a stroke away? Do we expect to get the ball close, or even sink it, from anywhere? Do we see an opportunity to score? This is important, because our perception will influence our expectation. Back to Henry Ford: do we *expect* to miss it? If so, the chances are that we will.

We must adopt a positive expectation about ourselves as putters. First, we need stop telling people, *including ourselves,* that we are poor putters. Many golfers have an unfortunate habit of doing this, which of course reinforces their perception. This is especially true after a simple or short putt is missed: how often in that situation do we immediately hear the player tell himself he is a 'bad' putter? The comment comes from exasperation, but the subconscious mind absorbs the message as information.

In the early days of computing, programmers would talk about 'garbage in, garbage out'. Charles Babbage, who was credited with inventing the first programmes, remembered being asked, 'If you put the wrong figures into the machine will the right answer come out?' The answer is obvious. In the same way, the self-image that our minds build is based on the external information they receive. **If we are sticking negative thoughts and comments into our minds, it should come as no surprise when we start to believe them.** On the putting green, those beliefs will increase the likelihood of missed putts.

I work with lots of golfers. Many of them are very critical of themselves, which naturally affects their confidence. One exercise I recommend is to ask them to find something positive to say, not only about the good strokes they make but also about the poor ones. If they roll it dead weight to the hole or sink a five-footer confidently, I ask them to say something positive such as, 'That felt great,' 'Feeling positive,' or, 'Great stroke.' We must obviously use words we are comfortable with.

Think of how you react when you are playing with a friend and they make a great shot. You are pleased for them and compliment them. Treat yourself exactly like you treat your friend and praise yourself. When you make a poor shot, a putt which is over-hit or a line poorly read, look for the positives in the shot. Avoid analysing the putt with negative language. Use phrases like, 'A good stroke but double-check the line next time,' or, 'That was fast, so slow the stroke down a little.' Using this kind of language stops negative thoughts; it is also useful technically when you come to the next putt.

The putting green is an unforgiving place. There is nowhere to hide. Therefore **it is important we make it a place we like and not a place we fear.** As we have seen, the putting surface is frustrating even for professionals. Out on the course they can shape shots from a variety of stances and hit power drives over three hundred yards, but on the putting green they lose more strokes than anywhere else. Every putt has a positional and, if you are playing the game professionally, a monetary value. It is no wonder that it becomes the place of the greatest stress on the course

Any engineer will tell you that where you have the greatest stress, you run the risk of experiencing a breakdown. **We need to avoid negative stress on the putting green and think only in positive terms.**

When a pilot and co-pilot prepare for a flight, they go through a detailed pre-flight safety check to make sure everything is done correctly and in sequence, thereby eliminating the chance of human error and finding any fault before it can become a problem. When we take a putt it is worth quickly doing a pre-shot mental check.

THE SIX RULES OF PREPARING TO PUTT

1. USE AFFIRMATIVE LANGUAGE

When we speak to a friend or family member who is going through a challenge, our natural instinct is to support them positively in words and action. Our language becomes affirmative as we seek to reassure them. We tell them that they will be fine, that they will overcome this obstacle and life will return to normal. When putting we need to apply this principle to ourselves: **We need to use positive, supportive language on the green and use positive affirmations when we sense any self-doubt entering our thinking**.

2. DON'T BE AFRAID OF THE PUTT

We have all missed short and relatively easy putts and immediately said, 'I knew I was going to miss that,' or, 'I didn't like the look of that.' More often than not we are trying to think ourselves out of the putt, because of the fear of missing it. Irrespective of how important a putt is – be it to break 70 for the first time in our lives, win a match or complete eighteen holes without a three-putt – **we must not be afraid of any putt.** It creates tension, the last thing we need on the green.

3. EXPECT TO MAKE IT

When we stand over a putt we need a positive expectation that we will make it. Think of how much we encourage our children with positive messages of encouragement and reassurance.

We should reassure ourselves with the same positive messages. **We should expect to deliver the perfect putt**.

4. STAY LOOSE

When we are tense our muscles tighten up. We become more rigid and jerky in our actions. When someone throws a small ball or beanbag at us, we catch it without thinking. Now imagine the same person is going to throw to us a very fragile and expensive antique vase! Suddenly we're tense. If we drop it there will be consequences. Now we're anything but physically relaxed. We will probably still catch it, but it won't be as pretty and comfortable as it would have been if we had been relaxed and fluid. **Putting requires that we are relaxed,** the stroke fluid and consistent. If we are having thoughts which contain self-doubt or negativity, then 'staying loose' is simply not going to be possible.

5. REMEMBER THE BEST PUTTS

Some years ago I was playing in a very close game. My partner and I were in the final match, which we had to win to give our team any chance of winning the series. We were two down. On the sixteenth green I had a long uphill putt, at least forty feet from just on the green, that broke about three inches from the left. Our opponents were lying seven feet away from the hole in two. If I missed the putt we would lose the match. I had played the same putt successfully earlier in the match but this was a totally different kind of pressure. I told my playing partner I was going to make it. I believed that I could make the putt. I felt confident that I would not falter or make a bad stroke. After reading the line and agreeing it with my partner, I stepped up and hit it exactly as I had imagined: the right amount of pace and the perfect line. It started taking the slight break, bearing right and, without drifting off line or running out of pace, it dropped perfectly into the centre of the hole. I just watched as it died into the cup with that wonderful noise.

We have all witnessed such putts from a long distance when we know – we just *know* – that the ball is going in. I felt a huge surge of relief, energy, joy and satisfaction at the same moment. I punched the air. My partner had a smile a mile wide. Our opponents were stunned. The pressure was now on them. They had considered the hole won. In the event they two-putted and lost. A magical moment at a critical point in the game. We were now one down with two to play. The momentum shift was amazing. The inner sense of energy flowing into our game was real and tangible. That putt remains to this day the best putt I have ever played. I felt it, saw it, called it and made it, under pressure. We won the seventeenth and the eighteenth, and the match.

When I recall that putt, those feelings of relief, energy, joy and satisfaction are relived, because my emotional connection to that event is stored in my memory. They energise me and make me feel confident for the challenge ahead. I recall that moment at times of stress both on and off the golf course. **Forget bad putts and selectively remember your great putts, especially before you go onto the course**.

6. AVOID BEING OVER-STIMULATED

Over-stimulation is one aspect of play in general, and putting in particular, which is often overlooked. Let me explain what I mean by being over-stimulated. Physiologically, we want our bodies to be in a relaxed state to perform at their best. We should arrive at the course in plenty of time. We don't want to be running late, driving too fast, changing in the car park and rushing to the first tee; if we do we'll find we're sweating and have a racing heart rate and a knot in our stomach. Does that sound familiar? This is what happens when we get stressed. This stress releases an adrenaline surge: we are over-stimulated and our relaxed state is a distant memory.

The more relaxed we are mentally, the more likely we are to perform without excess tension and at a higher level. Yet the paradox remains: how can we relax and play competitive golf where every stroke matters in relation to the outcome of the match? It is not simply a case of being indifferent to the outcome of the match. Winning is important. We play to win, even in a casual mid-week game with a friend. But we must avoid putting additional pressures on ourselves by letting our imaginations work against us. This happens when we allow ourselves to think that today is not our day! When we assume the worst, when we think we are jinxed, or that the stars are misaligned. Suddenly we imagine we are destined to have a bad day. We are not. Our imaginations can work for us or against us so we should **always imagine the best outcome over every putt.**

I would rather expect to make a putt and be surprised when it stays out than expect to miss it and be surprised when it drops! The sooner we become aware that we are in total control of our thoughts and the beliefs we hold about our ability as a putter, the sooner we will be able to adapt our thoughts, attitudes and thinking style to assist our progression towards becoming the best putter we can be.

When I discuss this with players a common response is, 'But it is unrealistic to believe you are going to make every putt." I always reply by pointing out that there is a big difference between belief and expectation. If we believe we are going to make a putt and we miss, we will question our beliefs and over time lose confidence in ourselves. If we *expect* to make the putt and we don't, the resulting disappointment will be easier to accept and the unrealised expectation will not damage our trust in our own judgement.

We become the putter we perceive ourselves to be. Believing we are a good putter and expecting to make a putt, keeps us in the perfect frame of mind to play well.

5

CONSIDER GETTING A LESSON

'You waste a lot of time going down blind alleys if you have no one to lead you.'

W Somerset Maugham

When was the last time you had a proper putting lesson from a professional? I would wager that most amateur golfers have never paid for a putting lesson in their lives. Surely putting is so simple we can figure out what to do on our own, can't we? Compare this to the amount of tuition we receive in other aspects of the game.

It's the same with our practice: we spend hours on the driving range with our drivers and wedges but no time at all on the putting green, practising reading the green, working on a pre-shot routine and developing a smooth stroke. **Yet the putter is the club we will use more often in a round than any other!**

Putting is deceptively simple. We think that we can putt, so why bother to practise? Who needs a lesson? Surely it is enough to watch golf on television, watch others on the green, get tips from a friend or, after a frustrating spell on the green, turn to a golf magazine or instructional manual that offers some answers? Or there's that plea after a poor putt, where we ask anyone who happens to be standing close, 'Can you see what I'm doing wrong?' Don't worry; someone always has a suggestion.

For most players, our putting stroke is essentially a work in progress. It periodically changes. We make adjustments to the grip, our stance or our follow-through. Because putting is about feel, we generally assume that if it feels right it must be fine. But if we're not making the putts we should, the chances are there is a technical fault. Things may feel fine, but it's possible that our set-up is wrong. If that is the case we end up continually adjusting our stroke to compensate, but never reaching the heart of the problem. The stroke will not be consistent. **We need to have complete confidence in our set-up and mechanics**.

Some golfers believe they have the ability to figure it out for themselves. PGA tour players Bubba Watson and Ricky Fowler do not have swing coaches but I am sure they get feedback from others they trust. In all my years of working with golfers I have yet to meet a player who can cure all their problems by themselves. Professional golfers, from the world number one to your local club pro, will at some time have someone look at their putting stroke to make sure it is aligned and that no bad habits have crept in. If Tiger Woods or Rory McIlroy believe they still have something to learn about putting, then surely that must apply to us too.

Bobby Jones won 13 majors, including the Grand Slam in 1930. Jones understood the importance of putting. In his early career he was recognised as a very gifted player but an unexceptional putter: his putting was the one aspect of his game that let him down and cost him championship wins.

Jones played in an age before computer-aided putter design. His putter was an old hickory-shafted club made around 1900. It had passed through a variety of owners before Jones acquired it. He affectionately named it Calamity Jane, and in his later career the club became a legend all of its own. This was due to his accuracy and his ability to sink critical long putts. Yet the putter was only 33½ inches long, weighed just 15½ ounces, and had a crack in the shaft, which was held in place with waxed binding thread. Jones said of his putter, 'It was rusty and sort of beat up, and no doubt had several owners before it ever got to me.' It was a club you wouldn't pick out of a barrel in a yard sale!

A photograph from the 1921 British Amateur Championship shows Jones with this putter. His feet are wide apart, he is crouched over the ball and he has a normal grip. But this conventional technique changed when Jones decided he needed a lesson, and went to the very best putter on the planet at the time.

Jones's putting teacher was Walter Travis, a somewhat serious-minded character who had taken up golf at the age of 34 in 1896, and then gone on to win the US Amateur Championship in 1900, 1901 and 1903. He was a self-taught golfer with a baseball grip and an unorthodox style. At 5'7" and 140 lbs, Travis realised that he had to compensate for his short stature, advanced years and lack of length off the tee by excelling on the green. Travis read everything he could about the game and practised the art of putting more than anyone before him. By his own admission he focused most of his time and energies on the concentrated practice of putting, and as a result became regarded as the greatest putter of his time. His delicate and deadly putting was acknowledged by players and journalists at the time. He later wrote:

> It is a matter of common knowledge that I have perhaps experimented with more kinds of putters than any other player in this country and should therefore be expected to have at least learned what not to do.

Travis retired when he was 54. In 1924, when he was 62, he watched Bobby Jones win his first US Amateur Championship at Merion. Travis said that Jones 'would never improve on his shot-making and his putting method was faulty'. Later that year Travis met with Jones at the Augusta Country Club. It is not clear whether this meeting was by chance or arrangement, but what is known is that Travis gave Jones a brief but very direct lesson.

According to Jones's biographer, Syd Matthews, this putting lesson 'changed the course of Jones's golfing history'. Travis instructed Jones to 'get his feet so close together that the heels almost touch' and to change his grip to a reverse overlap. He also told the young Jones to visualise a tack stuck in the back of the ball, and to drive that tack straight through the ball at impact. From 1924 to 1930 Jones rewrote the golfing record book, and he later acknowledged Travis's crucial contributions in his autobiography, *Golf Is My Game*.

Every serious golfer will learn from others in the pursuit of playing their best possible golf, but many weekend golfers refuse to do so. Only rarely do they go to the practice putting green before a round to try to get a feel for the pace of the greens. The practice green has a purpose. It is the closest we can get to finding out what the greens on the course are likely to do that day. If we are truly serious about our game we should invest time on the putting green. Our aim should be to walk off the practice putting green feeling more confident than we walked on to it. We should leave feeling connected to our stroke and in control, enabling us to putt with the confident expectation that we will make putts on the course.

Irrespective of how simple our putting technique is, **we should not discount the idea of taking a proper lesson.** Often a little advice is all we need to make a big difference. If just one aspect of our putting build-up and stroke contains an error that can be fixed, would it not be a worthwhile investment to do so? Like Bobby Jones with Walter Travis, it may take just one session to get things straightened out.

6

NO ROOM FOR SELF-DOUBT

'When you lip out several putts in a row, you should never think that means you are not putting well. When you're putting well, the only question is what part of the hole it's going to fall in, not if it's going in.'

Jack Nicklaus

There is an old joke about the American golfer who finally fulfils a lifetime ambition when he comes to play at the Old Course, St Andrews.

At the first hole, after four awful shots, he finally dumps the fifth shot in the water. Turning sheepishly to his Scottish caddy, he says, 'It's a funny old game.' To which the severe-looking caddy, without a smile, replies, 'Aye but it's not supposed to be.'

Unfortunately, there is nothing funny about putting. There are days when everything goes right. The hole is as big as a bucket. There is an inexplicable feeling of 'knowing' we're going to sink this putt. From a huge distance we will roll that perfect lag, dead weight. Then there are the other days. The opposite is true. We have no feel, no confidence. Suddenly an eighteen-inch putt seems as challenging as a twenty-footer. What is the difference? What causes us to go from being confident to full of self-doubt? We are still the same person, after all.

The difference is in our state of mind, or, to be more precise, in our personal level of expectation.

We all know the importance of a good opening hole. It is universally acknowledged that a good start is the foundation of a good round. A strong opening tee shot relaxes us. It puts a spring in our step and sets the tone for the round. Is it any wonder that the majority of professionals on the tour practise so intently with their driver? Tiger Woods always finishes his practice session by hitting the tee shot he requires off the first tee. We have all experienced the bad opening drive that clatters into the trees or heads off to the right or the left. It is unsettling and creates more concerns on the next tee box.

Once we reach the first green, the opening putt is as important as the opening tee shot, for it sets the tone for the rest of our day on the greens. That first putt can build or break our confidence. It gives us immediate feedback on our putting game at the start of our round.

I have often speculated that those who open their rounds with a one-putt will go on to take fewer putts in their round than those who open with a three-putt. Our success, or otherwise, can be seriously influenced by our experience on the opening putt. Our internal computer interprets that first putt as an indicator of how we are going to play from there on. For this reason, I believe we should **invest focused thought and attention in the detail of our first putt on the opening hole**.

I know from experience that when I putt well on the first hole, I unconsciously remove any niggling self-doubt that may be waiting to ambush me. On the other hand, when I only get the ball halfway to the hole, or jam it ten feet past, my lurking self-doubt immediately comes to life, claiming the putt as evidence that I am not going to putt well today.

Once we entertain self-doubt, we become uncertain. This is in stark contrast to those days when we start well and get a 'hot' streak going. In those circumstances there is no self-doubt. Confidence breeds confidence. I am sure we have all had this experience. As the US golfer Don January summarised it, 'The better you putt, the bolder you play.'

To putt well we need a mind full of conviction, without self-doubt or negative thoughts. We would not be human if we did not question ourselves or our ability to perform whatever task we set ourselves. This does not only apply to golf; it applies to any activity we undertake. But we have to remove the *inclination* to self-doubt or negativity. These feelings must be banished. This sounds simple enough, but in reality how do we do this?

Have you ever had to attend a party that you really didn't want to go to? In fact, you couldn't think of anything you would less like to do! As the party approaches, the negative thoughts begin: 'I really don't want to go,' 'It will be so boring,' 'I'll end up talking to some dull person.' In this situation we convince ourselves it is going to be awful and, more often than not, as long as we hold onto that belief, it will be. We settle into a pattern of thought in which we seek evidence to validate our expectation. Even if the party turns out to be fun and relaxed, with plenty of interesting people, our negative expectation will prevent us from fully enjoying ourselves: our expectation will shape our interpretation of events and experiences more than the evidence. In order to make the most of all situations, **we need to learn to manage our expectations**.

In golf, we should **always start by expecting to putt well**, for, whatever the outcome, our inner dialogue will align itself with our pre-putt expectation. If on the opening green we leave a twelve-foot birdie putt six feet short and our expectation was, 'Don't leave this short . . . it's a birdie putt,' then the poor outcome will be interpreted as, 'I have no clue what's going on with these greens,' or, 'I have no feel today,' or some other unhelpful response. Compare that with the reaction of the player who expects to play well. If his first putt is not quite what he intended, he will interpret the putt in as positive a manner as possible: 'Greens slower than I imagined,' 'I need to make a more committed putt next time,' 'Better here than on the eighteenth green.' What that player is doing is preserving his confidence by feeding back the positive aspects of the putt and giving no quarter to self-doubt.

Many a professional golfer's career has come to an end all too soon when they lost their confidence on the green, finding it replaced by indecision, uncertainty and in some cases even fear. This can happen to any golfer. We have discussed how Ben Hogan would hit green after green in regulation, but then freeze over the putt, and he's not the only major winner who knew his career had come to an end when he could no longer putt. Tom Kite, Johnny Miller and Sam Snead, amongst others, had to accept that irrespective of how close to the pin they could hit the ball, they could not get the job done on the green. The kind of pressure this repeated failure to finish a hole creates has been claimed as a cause of the 'yips' in some players.

When a player loses their certainty about a short must-make putt, they consciously or unconsciously develop a fear of the short putt. This fear gives way to a general nervousness which builds up over time, and this causes an involuntary muscular reaction: the 'yips'. In essence, if we become stressed or anxious, we stop being instinctive. We stop trusting the stroke that has served us well in the past and become too self-aware, acutely conscious of everything around us. We no longer believe in our ability to putt well under pressure.

Players and analysts have sought a neurological cause for the yips. The Mayo Clinic in the US carried out some research into the phenomenon, yet their findings suggested that the yips were more a psychological than neurological condition. In other words, their conclusion was that the yips were not caused by physical deterioration; rather that it was 'in the mind'.

We should take encouragement from the fact that two world class, major-winning players who admit to having had the 'yips' both overcame the phenomenon: Tom Watson and Bernhard Langer. Langer had to overcome the yips twice! This is encouraging because it demonstrates the old adage that anything we can learn we can unlearn. By adopting a strategic approach to their problem, both players found a way to overcome what could have been a career-ending challenge. In our own way, if we struggle with self-doubt on the greens, through good preparation and mental control, we can do the same.

PERCEIVE

7

BELIEF BEFORE BEHAVIOUR

'You have to expect things of yourself before you can do them.'

Michael Jordan

I am convinced that to become a good putter we have to believe we will become a good putter. We will only perform to the level of our own self-belief. I am not suggesting that we improve simply by believing, but to become the best putter that we are capable of becoming we must believe in ourselves.

A shift in belief creates a change in behaviour. When we believe something about ourselves, we automatically make adjustments to align how we act and perform with what we believe. The brain is the source of many of our actions, and performance skills based on physical ability are ultimately controlled by the brain. The motor muscle skills involved in taking a putt are initiated through the receptors in our nervous system, and the fine-tuned physical responses are overseen and coordinated by our brains. So if our brain believes we are good a putter, it will seek to realise that belief in our putting stroke. I have met players who scoff at this and say that putting is a mechanical action that can be learned. But I explain that, while it's true some things can be learned, the belief that our own ability *will* make the difference when we seek to move to the next level is not something we learn, it is something we *adopt*.

I have seen this in action time and again in the world of corporate training and development. Most training initiatives follow an established pattern. Imagine a company where the management decides to introduce a 'customer experience' initiative. The whole business is dependent on its customers and their return business, but there have been concerns about the way that customers have been treated. The management wants the staff to engage with the customers in a more positive and pro-active manner. They want the customers to feel valued and to receive a world-class level of service. The company decides to hire an external consultancy which specialises in this area of training, and the external consultants identify the behavioural changes needed to change the staff's approach to customers, and to increase customer satisfaction and return business. It is a thorough exercise, from examinations of the intellectual approach to customer management through to practical suggestions such as improving the friendliness of staff.

On paper, in the training room and during the various role-play exercises, all the changes seem to make perfect sense and appear eminently achievable. However, as anyone who has ever taken part in a project like this knows, such an exercise can only succeed if the staff believe in the value of the behavioural changes they are being asked to make. If the staff don't believe in the project, then nothing will change. During the first few days back on the shop floor, they may smile a little more. They may introduce themselves more frequently, repeat the stock phrases that were suggested in the classroom simulations. But before long there will be a return to past behaviours. A few employees will have genuinely tried, but the lack of support from their colleagues will have made them feel they were putting in far more effort than everyone around them, so they too will revert to the way things have always been done. This is a pattern repeated over and over, by retailers, hoteliers, restaurateurs and other customer service companies around the world. Nothing changes because the old beliefs remain in place.

I have witnessed a similar phenomenon in public seminars. Experts on stage share their knowledge while a huge audience attentively takes notes. The subject may be starting a business, positively transforming their lives, making money or finding true love. The theory is explained, but very few of the audience go on to realise their dream. It is not because the knowledge they are given is flawed or the presenters are frauds; it is because an individual may do everything the presenter instructs but, deep down, they don't really believe in the change. The enthusiasm is not matched by a deep belief that they *can* be different. In these instances, rather than seeing setbacks as opportunities to receive feedback or relearn the lesson, the individual interprets difficulties as proof they were destined to fail.

Belief, in the final analysis, is a very personal thing. Too little and we are considered insecure or lacking in confidence; too much and we are arrogant or big-headed. **Successful people have a positive belief in themselves and their ability to achieve**. Their validation comes from within and from the right external influences, such as close friends and colleagues who affirm to them their positive self-image.

On the putting green we need to believe we are good putters. The more diligently we practise, the easier and more naturally that feeling of belief will sit within us.

8

THE RENTAL SET PARADOX

**'Tension is who you think you should be.
Relaxation is who you are.'**

Chinese proverb

Have you ever played golf with a set of rented clubs? Rentals can vary from the top-of-the-range brands to a mixed bag from questionable origins. A friend of mine once played at a very exclusive golf course in Las Vegas; his rental set was taken from its original Callaway packaging and placed in a brand new bag for him. This was a far cry from those places where they hand you a bag of clubs with names that sound like a well-known brand but clearly are not, or a hyperbolic moniker that is meant to inspire confidence but does anything but.

No matter the quality of the clubs we're given, the main challenge with a rental set is that they are not our usual, familiar clubs. They feel, look and sit differently. In such situations, our reaction is one of resigned acceptance: we have a built-in excuse for not playing well. Yet I have noticed that when I'm using rental sets I tend to swing more easily. Rather than trying to send the ball a couple of miles down the fairway, I become more concerned with hitting a good shot.

The rental set really begins to feel odd when we get to the first green and take hold of the putter for the first time. We probably make a few practice strokes to get a feel for the weight and balance; no matter how different it is from our normal putter we have no choice about using it. In this situation, we concentrate on making a good stroke and keeping the clubface square through the impact. In my experience when we do that we frequently find ourselves making a reasonable job of putting, in spite of having an alien club in our hands.

Many times I have seen players, myself included, perform significantly better with a rental set than they normally do with their own clubs. I call this **the rental set paradox**. The expectation is that we'll play worse with a poor or unfamiliar set of clubs, yet we don't. Why?

It may seem counter-intuitive, but I believe that when we play with unfamiliar clubs we relax rather than tense up. We simply accept that these strange clubs will not perform as well as our own. We do not play with the same expectation, and in so doing we take a huge amount of pressure off ourselves. Crucially, **when we relax, we swing more easily and more instinctively.**

This is especially true on the green. If we are using a strange putter, we are forced to concentrate on the swing and keep our head still. We reacquaint ourselves with the fundamentals of the stroke so often overlooked.

About thirty years ago I played a round of golf in Los Angeles, at a public course where the rental sets were Ping lookalikes. They were so brightly coloured, I worried I would get a headache if I looked at them for too long.

We set off from the first tee. The first iron I played from the rental set was an eight-iron. I told myself to swing easy and not to thump it. The ball flew high and far, jumping off the face of the club as though it has been shot from a rifle: I immediately decided that despite their name and their colour these were good clubs! For the rest of the round I swung easily; I couldn't believe how well I was striking the ball and how far the ball was flying. The putter was a copy of a Ping putter, though much lighter. At the time I favoured a heavy-headed putter; nevertheless I putted remarkably well with this lighter model. By the fifth tee I was playing so well I had determined to buy a set of these fantastic clubs as soon as possible!

These obscure clubs were hard to find but eventually I discovered some at a discount golf store. That was when I had second thoughts: as soon as I actually found the clubs, I began to talk myself out of buying them. They were ugly, way too cheap to be good quality, and would doubtless cause me some ridicule back home. Consequently, I blithely put that amazing round down to mere luck. Even though I had played well with the lookalikes, I couldn't imagine myself playing as well with them as I did with my Mizuno TP-9s back in London. But, sure enough, when I returned to Britain I just couldn't find the form on my home course with my own clubs that I had enjoyed on a public course with a dodgy rental set. (The next time I was in Los Angeles a few years later I tried to find them again without success!)

Now I think I understand why I played and putted so well with that inferior set of hire clubs. First, I had understandably low expectations. Second, I relaxed and adopted a 'what will be, will be' philosophy. This allowed me to concentrate on making a good swing over every shot instead of trying to knock the cover off the ball. Third, playing on an unfamiliar course, I devoted more thought to distance and course management, taking a little more time over each shot, managing the whole process, rather than just walking up, taking a cursory glance at the ball and hitting it without even properly aligning my stance.

I am sure many of you have had the same experience when using rental clubs. Unencumbered and relaxed, you surprise yourself with how well you have played. For all of us, this is not because the clubs are better or worse, but because they have the effect of freeing us to **concentrate on making a good swing, unencumbered by high expectations of what the outcome will be**.

We need to learn this lesson and apply it on the green. **Good putting is about being optimistic and relaxed, making a sound stroke with a positive expectation of success.** I know this is easier said than done, especially when faced with the challenge of a curling six-footer on the sixteenth green to keep the game alive. But the main challenge of the pressure putt is to stay relaxed and allow our stroke to remain consistent: that is where the mental game comes into play. We have to find a way to prevent the racing heart and the sweaty palms from creating self-doubt. We have to stop the anxious thought of things going horribly wrong seeping into our mind.

Such focused calm is not innate; it is learned. Indeed, **to be able to be quiet, confident and comfortable on the green, we have to practise being quiet, confident and comfortable off the course.** This is something I will return to in the Practice section of the book. For now it is sufficient to recognise that putting is not a reaction game, like football, cricket, baseball or tennis. In these sports, most events happen so fast that the response is instinctive: a pure, intuitive approach is required. In golf there is always time to think ahead, to plan the next move. In golf we can take a considered approach to every shot we make: there is always scope for our state of mind to influence the outcome. This is clearly an advantage, but it can create problems.

We have all seen instances, in many different sports, where a player has *too much* time to think. At such moments an individual can go from unconscious excellence to a state of uncomfortable self-awareness. Suddenly they miss the penalty kick, serve a double fault or misdirect the ball straight to an opposing player. This is a good demonstration of overthinking and becoming tight. The player's awareness of the pressure mounts, and different expectations of the outcome creep in. Quickly, the player loses their feel, their intuitive reasoning, and replaces it with mechanical conscious effort.

Despite our initial dismay at its inferiority or unfamiliarity, the rental set has the opposite effect. We don't have too high an expectation of how we are going to play. We relax and concentrate on the fundamentals of technique and feel, which is what we should be doing every time we stand over the ball.

The rental set putter that releases us from anxiety isn't a 'charmed' or 'lucky' club. It's a trigger for a more profound sub-conscious mental process that takes hold of us involuntarily, but which any golfer can master to improve their game. The truth of the matter lies in the rental putter itself: objectively, we know it's an inferior tool. On reflection, we soon come to the realisation that it is the archer and not the arrow that has the biggest impact on whether we hit our target.

9

GOOD DAYS, BAD DAYS

'Acceptance of what has happened is the first step to overcoming the consequence of any misfortune.'

William James

Ionce met a professional golfer and instructor who had been a European tour pro for many years. The highlight of his career was that he once shot 60 in a tour event. He was a keen student of the game and had a philosophical view of golf in general – and putting in particular. He told me that after a lifetime of playing golf he had come to realise that if you have good days then you will also have bad days. You can do everything right and shoot a poor number. Equally you can feel awkward over every stroke and still post a low score. That's golf!

This is a genuine mystery. On a given day we can putt beautifully without doing anything obviously different. And then on other days we feel disconnected: the putter sits like a lump of wood in our hands. There are few more agonising on-course experiences than losing all feel and confidence on the putting green, especially on a day when from tee to green we have been striking the ball well. When it happens, it feels as if we've never played the game before.

Such times are challenging to any player, but when we experience one of those dark days, **when our touch on the green deserts us, we**

need to take control of our emotional state and restore our feelings of self-confidence by reminding ourselves that, though rare and unwelcome, such days happen! We must have faith and trust in our abilities, and accept the outcome of every putt, good or bad. As the old pro told me, 'that's golf'. We should never lose hope or give up trying, but must have the wisdom to accept the ups and downs on the course and keep on trying to play our best in a confident way.

In spite of how it sometimes feels, we do not have bad days on the putting green because the universe is conspiring against us! Neither is it because we lack the ability to putt well. Sometimes it just happens. Often when do not make a good putt, we lose confidence in our stroke and stop trusting in our ability to read the line and manage the right pace.

There are a number of strategies we can adopt to manage such a day:

1. **Stay positive and do not stop giving your very best**. There's a small distance between a positive and a negative mind-set on a golf course. We can go from upbeat to despondent in a heartbeat: it just requires one bad drive, an ill-timed comment or a terrible putt. But it's up to us how we cope with these setbacks: our attitude is our responsibility; it is completely under our control. Nothing can affect our attitude and mind-set unless we allow it to, so our mental approach should not be influenced by our playing partners or opponents, the weather or the course conditions. We must maintain a positive perspective on the events and situations occurring around us. We must concentrate on our own game almost to the total exclusion of what anyone else is doing.

   If we three-putted the first four greens in the club championship, we still have a choice as we step onto the fifth tee: 'How do I feel about myself now?' The first four greens are behind us; they should be forgotten. **Let's apply the twenty-five yard rule: if we make a poor shot, we allow ourselves twenty-five yards to think about what we could have done differently – and then leave it behind us.** We consciously move onto the next shot. The bad putts are history, so we tell ourselves that for the rest of the round the putts will be good. We remind ourselves that we're a strong putter; we relax, trust our stroke and give ourselves a positive pep talk. We avoid that downward spiral which many golfers get into: it doesn't have to be that way. We take control.

2. **Don't try too hard.** I find that when players try too hard to make a putt, to read the line perfectly and strike the ball perfectly, they often introduce too much attention to the actions they are taking. Conscious pursuit of the game's fundamentals can tip over into anxious obsession. We work best when we allow ourselves to take a more intuitive, instinctive approach. If we are having a bad day on the greens I would suggest changing the routine – just slightly – for a few holes. This may help correct whatever error has crept into our game. Over the years I have seen players change their grips or speed up their pre-shot routine during a round in an attempt to stop the rot on the green – often to great effect. The change allowed them to be more instinctive and natural, and stopped them overthinking and trying too hard.

3. **A smile or a shrug of the shoulders can work wonders** to keep the emotions balanced. I'm very fond of the French shrug of the shoulders, which they combine with the rather fatalistic expression of 'C'est la vie!' It's a physical expression of the sentiment, 'It is what it is.' It reminds us that the milk has been spilt, and there is nothing we can do about it, so why bother getting upset?

4. **Remember how it felt to putt well**. There's no point over-analysing our putting stroke to the point of distraction and confusion. Putting is about feel and confidence. We must hold onto the memory of good putts and how they felt; think back to a day when we putted beautifully. When we remember all the putts we dropped dead centre into the cup, we don't recall how we were gripping the club or standing over the ball; what we remember is that we felt good over the shot. We need to reconnect with that emotional memory of good putting days, and allow that feeling to flow through our mind and body.

It can be hard not to feel overwhelmed when having a bad day on the putting green. I have known that feeling; it's very demoralising. We feel like the victim of some random injustice. There are days when we wish we were not there at all. We apologise to our playing partner for the way we've performed – and in doing so accept, consciously or otherwise, that the failure is intrinsic. We must avoid this unwitting reinforcement of the feeling that we are a bad golfer. Putting can be the cruellest aspect of the game, and can reduce even the strongest-minded person to feelings of inadequacy and despair – but only if we allow that to happen.

When I was twenty-eight, I was diagnosed with cancer and spent a few months in and out of hospital. The realisation of the fragile nature of life and my own mortality was a very sobering experience. It helped me put everything else into perspective, to appreciate what truly mattered in my life as opposed to the other stuff that was really of no consequence at all. I love golf as a game, and as a lifelong experience it has taught me a lot about myself and other people. There is nowhere to hide on a golf course and we see the measure of other people out there. It has become a great metaphor for life in general – but it is not life or death.

After I had made my recovery I returned to the golf course. My game was rusty. I was physically weaker; I had lost distance. I hit some truly awful shots but I was playing golf again and I remember thinking, 'This beats being in the cancer ward!' I determined never to get truly angry on the golf course again. In the same way in which I dealt with each day of my illness as a bonus, I taught myself to take each shot as it comes on the golf course. I was determined to do my best, but to try not to obsess about the outcome.

We should make the most of our time on the course. No matter the outcome, whether we take 24 putts or 42 putts, every time we play the game of golf we learn something. We need to accept both those rounds for what they are: enjoy the good round, let go of the bad round, and remember the positives we took from each one.

10

JUST A ROUTINE PUTT

**'A routine is not a routine if you have
to think about it.'**

Davis Love Jr

Different sports have different ways of judging winners. In high diving and gymnastics, certain routines are judged not simply on their execution but also on their degree of difficulty. A triple back-flip somersault from the high board will be acknowledged as a more demanding test of skill than a forward roll dive. To execute a dive with a high degree of difficulty the athlete needs to be very experienced and to have put in many hours in training. It would be extremely difficult for a novice to attempt the same manoeuvre because they don't have the skill or the experience. Golf may not involve somersaults and high dives but, in the same way, the most successful golfers are invariably those who have been the most diligent in their practice. As Lee Trevino put it, 'There is no such thing as natural touch. Touch is something you create by hitting millions of golf balls.'

Naturally some putts are more challenging than others, but the player who has practised regularly trusts their stroke and their reading of the line, so is more likely to be successful. When I work with golfers I ask them not to think of a putt as being easy or tough, but rather to see every putt as routine. Think about the physical act of putting.

Every putt is hit in the same way. You cannot do with a putter what you can do with the other clubs in your bag. All putts are hit in a straight line; it is the contours of the green that give shape to the line the ball takes. So if, from the perspective of the clubface, every putt is straight, then it is better to **think of every putt as being routine and straightforward.** This really helps removes unnecessary stress from the putt.

Of course, I'm not suggesting those forty-foot downhill putts you see during the Masters, with a big break one way or the other on the Augusta greens, are 'easy'. But there is a difference between a difficult putt and an important putt, for example a short putt for the course record. The former is technically challenging; the other is challenging due to its context. I know players who are wonderful lag putters. From long distances or off the green they can repeatedly roll the ball to within short distances of the hole. For them such putts are not difficult. Yet the same players, when faced with a dead straight two-footer, can convince themselves that It is a 'tough' putt. These are matters of perception and interpretation. **We do not help ourselves by saying a putt is difficult**. If we look at each putt as a routine putt we can concentrate on line and pace, without the added pressure of thinking, 'This is tough; I'll be lucky to get it close.'

I am aware that there are occasions when a three-putt looks a certainty: there are those times, especially from above the hole, when getting the ball within ten feet would be considered good. But, equally, our perception of the putt and the interpretation of its degree of difficulty is something we can manage. **If we truly believe a putt is hard or difficult, we are more likely to experience tension.** We are more likely to entertain self-doubt and force the shot rather than let it flow. We are also preparing our own justification in case we fail. Therefore **we must trust ourselves to assess and play putts without labelling them 'tricky', 'hard', or 'difficult'.**

There is a paradox. If viewing a putt as 'difficult' can affect our confidence or ability to remain relaxed, should we also avoid labelling a putt as 'easy'? My response is simple: no. Anything we can say or think that helps us relax and that builds our confidence is a good thing. **We must seek to avoid negative thoughts and emotions.** I have always felt that the perfect mental state for the putting green and the course in general is neutral or slightly positive, irrespective of what happens. The more we can keep ourselves in a positive frame of mind, the better. The more we can look at every shot as being a routine shot that we know we have made during practice, the better placed we will be to succeed on the green.

We will find it easier to treat every putt as customary if we already have a putting routine. Watch tour players on the putting green during a tournament. No two golfers have exactly the same routine. They may go through the same checklist before the shot (gauging pace and break), but when it comes to how they read the putt, how they lay down their ball, the number of practice putts they take (if any) and the time they take before they make the actual stroke, they will almost certainly differ. And generally speaking, these routines, developed during thousands of hours on the practice green, do not change. The very familiarity of the routine is a marvellous way of helping a player stay relaxed. Having a putting routine gives a sense of comfort, making it easier to put the body on autopilot and make the best possible stroke.

We should create our own putting routine, not copy other people. By all means, we can watch others and look for aspects of their routine we think are helpful. It might be the length of time taken over the read, or the number of practice putting strokes taken. Our pre-shot routine is rather like our signature. We may be using the same letters of the alphabet to construct our name, but the way we lay it down on paper is unique. There is no right way to prepare ourselves to putt, but there is a best way for each of us, and that is the way which we find most comfortable.

For a long time, I had no real routine – at least none that I was conscious of. I used to spend a lot of time reading some putts but less on others. Sometimes I would take four or five practice strokes; other times a cursory glance, step up and hit without any pre-shot ritual. Unsurprisingly, I was inconsistent on the green, but at the time I didn't see the connection.

One day when I was playing with a friend we agreed we would go round as quickly as possible. There was no one in front of us. We played 'ready golf'. You play the ball as soon as you get to it. Even on the green! It was a case of look at the hole, pick your line and hit it.

The result was amazing. I putted as well as I had done for a very long time. I realised that I was playing instinctively, intuitively. I was not over-analysing and over-thinking. This experience inadvertently helped create what has become my putting routine. The change to my pre-shot build-up made me feel more connected to the putt; I was simply 'getting on with it' and not examining too many factors. That day I putted with more confidence than usual, and did not think of putts as being easy or hard; rather I saw them simply as shots I trusted myself to play.

We need to treat every putt as a routine putt. We need to detach ourselves from the outcome of the shot. The ball is either going to go in or it is not going to go in. The result will not be apparent until the stroke is played. In the end, putting is all about picking the right line and hitting it with the right pace. Having a pre-shot routine will help us focus more on the line and pace, and less on control or outcome.

11

MAKE THE NEXT ONE

'I am an optimist. It does not seem too much use being anything else.'

Winston Churchill

When I am in Scotland I sometimes play golf with a group of guys on a Sunday morning. One of them is a very good golfer, but his game is destroyed by his inability to hole short putts. His long putting game is fine but the short putt has him completely flummoxed. I have watched him closely. His pre-shot routine looks fine, with nothing obviously at fault. He does everything correctly. But when it comes to the actual putt he jabs at the ball and can often end up further past the hole than the original putt. It destroys his game. A short putt missed can be agonising, and takes a while to forget. It can be particularly damaging in match-play. I know in the case of this friend it stays in his mind and works away at his confidence.

We have all been there. It is early in the game. We're still sounding our opponent out. We have a little tester for a half. We're thinking, 'I hope he gives me that!,' but the opponent is silent. He wants to see what we're made of. We have to putt. It slips past. It rattles our confidence and self-doubt begins to creep in. We must avoid this. In truth, the missed putt is now simply a detail, a historical footnote to the match. If we really want to, we can return to it in the club house when we're reviewing the game, but while we're out on the course we need to forget about it, because there is absolutely nothing we can do about it.

The only putt that matters now is the next one. Think back to the twenty-five yard rule. In the time it takes to walk to the next tee, we must transfer all our focus to the next shot. Stay in the present, not the past. We have all watched world-class professionals on television miss a short birdie putt and then too quickly and unbelievably miss the return. It is almost inevitably due to the player not taking their time, not investing in the same pre-shot routine for the equally important return putt. When we miss a short putt that we expected to sink, we experience an emotional response: anger, frustration, injustice, rage – or all of them together! It is best to let that first response fade before proceeding. This is why we must stick to our pre-shot routine on every putt, especially when we are upset or angry at having missed a short one. Otherwise we increase the chance of another miss, which will further damage our confidence.

The friend of mine who misses so many short putts only gives his pre-shot routine a chance on his first putt. The rest of the time, lacking in confidence and uncertainty, he simply rushes through the next shot (or two) to get the ball in the hole as quickly as possible and get off the green. It is hard to watch, and he is only compounding the problem by not giving each putt his full attention, plus the fact he genuinely believes he is probably going to miss it.

We all know the feeling as an important short putt appears to be getting more difficult with each passing moment. The pressure builds, as our previously intact confidence falters. We end up experiencing different emotions dependent on the outcome. If we make the return we are relieved. If we miss it we have a sense of dread. Will it be one of those days?

This has as much to do with physiology as psychology. Stress or worry will make us speed up – it is a mild (yet significant) adrenaline response – which is why taking time out and being more deliberate on important short putts will in the long run prove more rewarding than simply stepping up quickly.

Often when I have missed a putt and the hole is finished I will retake the putt to see if I can improve on what I did. On the second occasion the putt is invariably better. Yes, I now have the benefit of knowing more about the line and the pace of the green, but the real reason the putt is better is because it is struck with more confidence. The putt doesn't have the same importance, so the pressure is off. I can relax and play, with no worries about missing it. Imagine if we took all our putts with that same attitude! **We must be confident and stroke the ball with an expectation that we will make it – but without attachment to the outcome**. If we do this I believe we will see a significant improvement in our game.

At the heart of silent mind putting lies the concept of 'staying in the present' – the ability to give no thought to the past or to the future. If we make a putt, that's good. If we miss a putt, we learn whatever lesson the miss taught us but then don't dwell on it. We bring our focus back to the next shot. **A positive approach is critical to putting to the best of our ability. This is not a technical challenge. It is a mental state. We create it. We control it.**

Anything we do that is unhelpful to our performance should be avoided. Negative self-criticism, blaming our clubs, blaming our opponent, getting angry with ourselves: these are all things we need to avoid. The best way to stay in the moment is to give our full attention to the putt that we are about to play, calmly and in a relaxed manner. How far is it? What is the line? How much pace will I use? We should go through this routine with the positive expectation that we are going to make a good shot.

The following exercise can be helpful if practised regularly:

SINK IT ▶

1. Sit properly and quietly in an upright chair. Breathe slowly and deeply. Allow yourself to relax physically.
2. Silently count back slowly from ten to one. Continue to be as physically relaxed as possible. When you reach one, keep breathing slowly and methodically. Allow your mind to empty. Think of nothing at all.
3. See yourself on the putting green with a three-foot putt. After viewing the scene in this detached way, change your point of view to your first-person view of the putt. (You are now standing over the ball.)
4. Be aware of how relaxed you have become. Transfer this state of relaxation to the you who is taking the putt. Take the putt and see it run three feet past the hole.
5. Now *feel yourself remaining perfectly calm.* You are an observer to the missed putt. You are not angry or thinking negative thoughts.
6. Line up the next putt with a positive expectation you will make it.
7. Hole the putt.
8. Repeat stages 4 to 7 a few times.
9. When you are finished, allow your mind to empty again. Think of nothing.
10. Silently count forward from one to ten. When you got to ten, open your eyes. The exercise is over.

The purpose of this visualisation is not better shot-making. It is about emotional detachment: staying in the moment without negative feelings. Sometimes when I have tried this exercise with one of my clients he will say, 'I don't want to visualise ever missing a putt. I don't want that image in my head.'

My reply to that is, 'Do you ever miss short putts?'

'Yes.'

So the fact he has never visualised missing a short putt hasn't stopped him missing one! The purpose of this visualisation is to stop a player being emotionally hijacked – which is more likely on the green than anywhere else. We must be aware of the danger caused by a negative emotional response (anger) and have a clear strategy to prevent it.

12

PLAY IT IN YOUR HEAD FIRST

'Visualisation lets you concentrate on all the positive aspects of your game.'

Curtis Strange

I am a firm believer in the power of positive visualisation. This is a technique that allows us to imagine the outcome we want before the actual event takes place. I ask my clients to apply it to their golf shots. The technique puts the image of success into the mind, so that when a player goes to take the actual shot, the subconscious mind associates that image with the real-world situation being played out on the course. The golfer has a positive image of themselves successfully completing the shot they are about to take. That image boosts confidence and raises expectation. Before I putt, I visualise the ball going into the hole. **I play the shot in my head before I play it for real. I never visualise myself putting; I visualise the ball rolling towards the hole and going in.**

When I started playing golf I used to putt like many other golfers. I would hit the ball more in hope than expectation. With my long experience of working with golfers, I now associate such an approach with a lack of positive expectations or self-belief. **On the putting green confidence is _the_ key factor which makes the difference.** Without it, we really are relying on luck – and, as we all know, luck is a fickle friend!

The majority of golfers hope to make a good putt when they stand over the ball. But there is a big difference between hope and belief. Few golfers really *believe* their putt will be good. If a golfer misses a lot of short putts over a period of months, it will be no surprise to find their expectations have declined as a result. But as expectations dwindle, so does confidence – and form. The process of negative expectations leading to poor putting, back to negative expectations, and so on, is a vicious circle.

If we wait until we begin to putt well before we are willing to think of ourselves as a good putter, we may be in for a very long wait. If our confidence is shackled to experience, we will find it hard to escape the downward spiral in which poor experience leads to low expectation and a drop in confidence. There is an old saying: 'Fake it until you make it.' In other words, we should act and behave as if we are successful before – and until – we are. This belief will lift our self-image into one that is more positive; the lift in confidence will make our expectations more consistent with our actual capacity to succeed.

The theory may sound like wishful thinking but it is based on the simple premise that **we act in accordance with our dominant thought**. If our dominant thought is one of success, we tend to see the positive and we do not get bogged down by the negative. Conversely if our dominant thought is negative, we tend to see the evidence that validates that belief. Practically, this means that if a person who is confident and has positive expectations three-putts on the first green they will quickly forget their poor play and move on. Moreover, they will seek to put a positive spin on it: to see it as an opportunity to re-examine the speed of the green or the degree of break. The negative thinker will do the exact opposite. They will see those three putts as further evidence that they are not a particularly good putter. For the rest of that round this lack of confidence will undermine their stroke.

When I explain this to clients individually, or to the groups of golfers I speak to, I am often asked if what I am saying boils down to, 'Irrespective of how you are playing on the course, think positively and believe you are a good putter.' The simplest answer to that question is, '*Yes*.'

Of course, thinking positively isn't quite as easy as a simple 'yes' suggests. The truth of our predicament may have become clear to us, but it does not reveal an easily flicked internal switch that will enable us to shift from a negative mental state to a positive one at will. Over time we can greatly improve our mental game in golf, but just like the physical game, doing so requires discipline and practice. We need to learn techniques that enable us to develop and maintain confidence irrespective of what is happening on the course. The exercises and tips I have included throughout this book will help us to develop our positive equilibrium whatever the game situation.

Golf is a 'thinking time' sport. We play with a stationary ball. We always have time to analyse the shot, consider it and **think *before* we play**. Think then act. A friend of mine once played in an invitational golf day where each four-ball included one player from the senior tour. The format was a Texas Scramble. His professional was Maurice Bembridge, a European Tour winner and four-time Ryder Cup player. On one hole my friend had hit the best drive, and his ball was selected to be played by all of the players. He marched up to his ball and was about to play it when Maurice came up beside him and said to him, 'Don't do anything in a hurry.'

My friend still thinks this was one of the best pieces of advice he has ever been given on a golf course. For the rest of the round he watched Bembridge play. Bembridge was not a slow player, but he never did anything in a hurry. He considered his options. He thought about what he was going to do and then he played. If we can marshal our thoughts in a constructive way then it stands to reason that it can only make things better.

The second aspect of a pre-shot mental strategy is to approach and **play every shot with the confident expectation of perfect execution**. In short, we do not entertain any doubt about our read of the putt or our stroke. I appreciate that this is much easier said than done, but in the final analysis **we need to trust ourselves on the greens**. A good habit to establish is to practise before going onto the course to play. Many golfers don't take the time to warm up or go through any putting drills before they play. They simply head off to the first tee. Players then wonder why they putt poorly, and spend the rest of the round tinkering with their putting stroke.

On the course is the last place to experiment with our putting stroke. It immediately creates tension in our play. We find ourselves trying too hard to control the mechanical aspects of the swing and, as we do so, the sense of 'feel' reduces, and the club ends up feeling like a lump of timber. Our confidence comes from repeated success, memories of positive achievement, being free from distraction and a routine that we completely trust. Anything we can do to build confidence will help. Consider some of my recommendations from elsewhere in the book: practise with purpose; use positive self-talk; be willing to change your putter; treat every putt equally; develop a pre-shot routine; be kind to yourself when you play a poor putt; and step up to every putt with the expectation of 'confident execution'. Such simple steps will build a positive mind-set that will develop our mental resilience.

Improving our mental game means developing positive expectations. In the absence of facts, we have to rely on faith, which finds its origin in hope. We hope to become better putters but have no real evidence that we are in fact doing so. There is no scientific test that will determine our potential on the putting green, no magic potion to drink or mantra to recite; there is only a belief that we can get better. Without that belief, we will perform to the level of our expectation. The catalyst of hope is a positive mental attitude.

What does a positive mental attitude consist of? *Determination* to succeed, *commitment* to practice, *encouragement* to ourselves on the green, *enthusiasm* to learn, *control* of our anger when things go wrong: all these will contribute to increased positivity; they are the bedrock of the mental game.

Though they invariably understand the concept, and can appreciate the value in theory, few players actively seek to develop their mental strengths. Some assume because they understand it they can *do* it. Understanding is one thing; it's another thing to perform on the course when the pressure is real. **The best players under pressure are naturally those with the most experience of playing under real pressure.**

However, we now know that visualising on-course pressure situations, where we 'see' ourselves performing confidently under this pressure, will give us a competitive edge on the course when those pressure situations are for real.

13

PACE

**'Trust yourself.
You know more than you think you do.'**

Benjamin Spock

Getting the pace of a putt right is a critical skill. It is especially important on the longer putts, where we can consistently reduce the length of our second putts if we can get the pace right. In the long run this will result in fewer putts per round.

As we all know, no two golf courses have greens which behave in exactly the same way. On every golf course the greens change from day to day, even throughout the day, depending on the weather, the wind and their preparation by the green staff. Many courses now have sophisticated greens equipment, making the greens even slicker and faster on competition days! There is always a variation in the speed to be found on greens we play on as amateurs. But if we think these greens are fast, we would not believe the speed of the greens major tournaments are played on. How many times have we heard a commentator remark, 'I don't think the viewers at home have any idea how fast these greens are'?

After the Masters finishes at Augusta, journalists who have covered the tournament can take part in a ballot to play the course on the Monday. Graham Spiers was covering the tournament for the *Glasgow Herald*, and he filed a report on his experiences. His story included the following remark: 'I was delighted to be on the green in regulation two and off again in three!'

I have played on championship greens and they are a completely different experience. The pace depends on the geography and, of course, the green staff's preparation. We have to be able to adapt our touch to the nature of the greens we are playing. The stroke we use to move the ball twelve feet on our home course may on another course send it six or twenty-four feet. So we need to rely more on feel than mechanics.

Experiments have been conducted with mechanical putting devices to test the roll and quality of strike on a ball. Even these do not produce exactly the same result every time. Research has shown that even from a few feet they have a dispersal pattern and, like humans, miss the hole now and again. So if a putting machine is imperfect, I think we should accept the likelihood that our own stroke is not going to repeat exactly every time we putt. From this realisation, it follows that the pace of the putt is as important as the line that we take. If the longer putt drops, that is a bonus, but the important thing is to take the ball close enough that the next putt should be a formality.

A putt hit on the perfect line which pulls up eight feet short can be more damaging to our confidence than a putt which is slightly off line but is dead weight. The fact that the weight was right and it is close is a great confidence-builder at the beginning of a round. The opposite is equally true. Start a round with a three-putt on the first green, and the experience can (if we allow it to) affect our confidence. If we are not in control of our emotional state that will probably set in motion the negative mental process that leads to tension and poor form.

When we putt we need to be authoritative and self-assured about our stroke. Self-assurance is important because without it we are just guessing what the green is going to do. When we guess the feel, our stroke generally becomes more mechanical and less intuitive.

We need to be aware of the potential pace of the green. We must not simply assume it will be similar to other courses in the area. We need to be sensitive to all of the conditions around us. When we walk onto a green, we should always mark and lift our ball. We should sense the firmness of the green. Does it give? A firm green is going to be faster than a soft green. Is the grass cut short or is it a little longer than average? Has it been rolled? Shorter rolled grass is faster than longer grass. Is it wet? Is there sand on the green from bunker shots? Any impediments on the green, no matter how small, will slow down a ball. We need to form an instinctive opinion as to how fast or slow we think the green is. Throughout our golfing careers we walk onto hundreds, perhaps thousands of putting greens. When we walk onto the green, our memories of similar conditions will intuitively give us an immediate sense of the speed and pace we need for the putt.

PRE-ROUND PRACTICE GREEN SUGGESTIONS ▶

1. Drop three balls and putt to three different targets. The purpose is to see the line, quickly trust it and play by feel alone.
2. Rather than using the putter, roll some golf balls underhand at one of the practice flags. I find this an excellent method of feeling distance and the kind of weight we need to make with the putter. It also stops us thinking about swing mechanics, and forces us to be more instinctive.
3. Make a point of 'feeling' confident with each putt; don't just absent-mindedly hit some balls and hope a few go in. We need to engage our emotional feeling of being a great putter.
4. If we miss a few short putts, let's not worry about it; they don't count! We should take the view: better on the practice green than on the course.

We've all had days when we left every putt dead. We had the pace of the greens nailed, and no matter where we were on the green we just felt we were going to get it very close. This is more a mental than a mechanical skill. It requires being in tune with our intuitive sense of feel. This sense of feel is a subtle aspect of putting. Some people are more connected to it than others. We all have it but few of us access and trust it.

If we trust our feel for the green and go with it, we will be much more likely to make a confident stroke. How often have you heard a commentator describe a golfer as a 'feel' player, or in a post-round interview heard a golfer say that he had the 'feel' of the greens today? That player has achieved a heightened sense of awareness that subconsciously influences their game and their ability to play a specific shot. Some of the best putters in the world were unconventional in their technique, but they were successful because they trusted their instinctive 'feel'.

I would like to recommend another visualisation exercise for you to try:

SEE IT – MAKE IT ▶

Think of a green on your home golf course. It can be a green that you like playing, or perhaps one that you have difficulty with. Now, sit comfortably in an upright chair, relax and breathe normally.

1. Count backwards from ten to one; take about two minutes to do this, leaving a ten or fifteen second gap between numbers.
2. Empty your mind. Breathe deeply. Relax.
3. Imagine your chosen putting green. Be sensitive to the green. Mark your ball. Be aware of the firmness of the green, the moisture on the surface, the greenness of the turf, the length of the grass.
4. Before you make a putt, allow yourself to feel the pace simply by employing your senses: touch, smell and sight.
5. You have a putt that is eight feet from the hole. Visualise the ball going squarely into the hole. When you take your practice stroke, look at the hole, not the ball. *Fix your eyes on the hole, not the ball. Remember the*

SEE IT – MAKE IT (continued) ▶

hole is the target, not the ball. Then, when comfortable, visualise taking the actual putt with your eyes still fixed on the hole. See the ball dropping cleanly into the hole.

6. Repeat this putting sequence six or seven times.
7. Slowly count back from ten to one until you are fully aware.

This exercise encourages us to play by feel and not by sight, and to trust our swing and not interfere with the position of the clubface through the swing. Once mastered at home, the next step is to take it onto the practice green and repeatedly putt looking only at the hole and not at the ball. This will build our confidence in our ability to putt without looking at the ball. I recommend this visualisation drill, particularly after a round when we find ourselves having a bad time with pace.

I now play about ninety per cent of my putts looking down the line of my putt at the hole, and rarely at the ball. The result has been more putts on line and fewer push or pulled short putts. If we are in the habit of pushing or pulling short putts, trying this technique for a while can work wonders.

Everyone has the capacity to be a better putter. More than any other aspect of the game, the simplicity of putting means that confidence, instinct and feel are crucial. Putting is highly susceptible to changes in our mental state. As I often tell my clients, and have mentioned elsewhere in this book, if our mind tells us we are a poor putter, it's an odds-on certainty that we will be.

14

PRACTISE ON THE PRACTICE GREEN

'There is no glory in practice, but without practice, there is no glory . . .'

Anonymous

The title of this chapter may seem like a statement the obvious. But in my experience few golfers really use the practice putting green for 'real' practice – if they use it at all. When most people go to the practice green before a round of golf, it is to get the feel of the greens and to find some rhythm for their stroke, they are almost always simply warming up, without any conscious notion of 'practising', let alone a 'practice routine'.

I compare the notion of a pre-game warm up and a diligent practice session to the way that some students spend their time during the academic year. The diligent student conscientiously studies throughout the term in the knowledge she will sit exams at the end of term. The 'pre-game warm up' student skips classes and then crams for two days solidly before the exam. The diligent student will have a proper depth of knowledge, command and understanding of the topic, while the crammer will have a head full of facts and figures that may get him through the exam but are unlikely to amount to genuine knowledge a few days later.

If the crammer passes the exam, his feeling will be one of relief at 'getting away with it – again'. If he fails, there will be frustration and the knowledge that he'll have to re-sit. The diligent student is more likely to have passed, but if she has failed she will find it easier to identify the gaps in her knowledge and address them before the retake.

One of the most effective ways of improving our putting is through purposeful practice. The professionals have long known that the key to winning is success on the green, and consequently it is there that they spend a lot of time in practice, going through drills to enable them to develop a pre-putt routine and a stroke that they trust. The short game is the area of the game that they practise the most. The professional requires a stroke they can repeat under tournament pressure.

If we practised our putting diligently for thirty minutes every day, six days a week, I think we can safely assume that we would develop a more consistent stroke and considerably improve the quality of our play. The more we practise our pre-shot routine and putting stroke, the more comfortable we will become with it. We will achieve the easy familiarity and the solid confidence that accrues naturally as a consequence of repetition. Our shot will become more automatic, comfortable and instinctive.

When tour professionals discuss their practice putting drills, their efforts often appear to border on the extreme. They make themselves sink fifty consecutive four-foot putts. If they miss one, they go back and start all over again. They can spend hours on the green doing the same thing over and over and over again.

The average club golfer plays for fun, not for money, titles, sponsorship and fame. We don't necessarily have the time to practise like the tour pros. Nonetheless, I think all of us also want to win. Winning is a more pleasurable experience than losing. If we really want to win, we need to act like the diligent student and not the last-minute crammer.

Diligent practice on the putting green is the most neglected part of the amateur's game. A few short putts, to get the pace of the green, before going to the first tee, without following a proper drill, is not the best preparation to play our best golf. I used to fall into this category. Like most golfers, I found hitting full shots much more satisfying and I had little evidence to support the notion that the time I spent on the putting green made any significant difference to my game on the course. Now I am able to identify the flaw in my approach: I did not practise with any purpose when I was on the putting green. I would concentrate over ten or fifteen shots and just hope a number of them would go in so I could take that game onto the course.

My putting did not begin to improve until I found a putter I truly loved (see Chapter 3) and took the time to practise and find a stroke that I had total faith in. Then I spent time on the practice putting green, going through a number of confidence-building drills and focusing on hitting the ball down the intended line with as little uninvited input as possible. By 'uninvited input' I mean consciously opening or closing the putter face, abandoning my normal pre-shot routine, or just having a stab at the ball – any unwelcome changes to my stroke.

It is helpful to be consistent with our pre-match practice routine. Before a competition round, professionals go through their putts in a particular order. We should do the same. Start with some long putts to get a feel for pace, then short putts to build a good feeling for making a confident stroke. If there is a putt that historically we have had trouble with, such as a short putt with a little break, or lagging long-distance putts, we should practise a few of these, so that when we go to play them on the course we will have some feel for the shot.

Pre-round practice helps eliminate unwelcome inputs – such as low confidence and low expectations – that will make our play self-conscious and too mechanical. All these thoughts and feelings expose us to self-doubt, making us anxious about the one aspect of our game about which we should be confident and positive in order to perform at our best.

Mastery of any activity is difficult, and putting is no different. There are days when all feel and sense of confidence abandons us, and, no matter how hard we try, the ball refuses to go in the hole. Even the shortest putt becomes a major challenge. It is an awful feeling, and every player has at some time in their golfing life experienced it – some more than others! Then there are days when our putter feels like a *Star Wars* light sabre that enables us to putt with the full knowledge that we can make just about any shot we wish. Long putts die right beside the hole and the odd one or two drop on the final turn. Short putts never leave the line from the moment they are struck and fall firmly into the middle of the cup. Some days we are hot and other days we are cold.

There is not always a logical explanation. But I believe that in many cases such days are determined by the early events of a round. For example, a run of early successes on the green can convince us we have the feel of the greens, while a lack of confidence at the subconscious level can be brought to the surface as a consequence of a missed putt early in the round, allowing us to begin doubting our own ability.

If we have a good putt on the first green our game is given a shot of confidence. If we hit a poor putt our confidence, which may be fragile at the best of times, can be destroyed. The fastest practical way we have of building and shoring up our confidence is to put in time on the practice putting green, repeating purposeful drills in complete concentration. This will help us achieve a confident, positive stroke on every putt – especially those early putts out on the course.

The more we practise, the more we are able to tell ourselves on the course, and especially when the pressure builds, that we have played this exact putt before. Practice allows us to see each putt for what it is: *just another routine putt.* We're all familiar with the old expression, practice makes perfect. I would say that **purposeful practice makes perfect**.

For almost three decades, K. Anders Ericsson and his associates at Florida State University have been conducting research on peak performance. Their results clearly indicate that 'deliberate practice' under expert supervision is far more important to success than notions such as 'innate talent' or 'luck'. As their research demonstrates, **the talented individual without practice fades; the lucky individual shines once; but the person who diligently practises will in time out-perform them both**.

In his best-selling book *Bounce*, Matthew Syed, a former British table tennis champion, argues very convincingly that in complex sporting activities, including tennis, golf and chess, a 'natural talent' is of pretty low importance. Because of the complicated wiring of the brain, the neural pathways that enable us to perform complex movement or strategic thinking only work after massive amounts of purposeful practice. Often the outcome of years of intense practice is mistaken for natural talent. In fact, the most common trait that high achievers share is a willingness to work and train harder than others.

A belief in the value and benefit of this training is the foundation of their confidence, not some vague ingrained sense that they are naturally superior.

When we read the biographies of many of the great players of the past or on the professional circuit today, we might be amazed by the extraordinary amount of practice they put in. The overwhelming evidence is that diligent, purposeful practice and hard work bring success.

15

REMEMBER THE
BASIC PRINCIPLES

**'Don't practise until you get it right.
Practise until you can't get it wrong.'**

Anonymous

The basic form of a good putting stroke has one simple mechanical movement. The club head must strike the ball in such a manner that it sends the ball down the intended line of the putt. The act of putting is a very simple movement when we think about it in these terms. It's also simple when compared with the complicated physical movements executed in other sports: leaping over hurdles at speed; diving to volley an intended passing shot in tennis; curling a forty-yard pass over two defenders in football; being tackled by three hefty opposition players in rugby without losing the ball – and usually doing all of these with a lot of background noise. None of this happens when we putt.

When we putt we stand perfectly still. There is a respectful silence from spectators and opponents. We strike the ball with a club specifically designed for that purpose, across some of the smoothest surfaces in sport. What could be easier? Ironically it may be the very simplicity of putting that causes us to forget the basics and spend the rest of our lives in search of golf's Holy Grail, the secret to perfect putting. There are hundreds of books of putting instruction. The putting stroke has been examined, deconstructed, reconstructed, forensically analysed and studied as much as is humanly possible. Every instructor has his own view as to what is truly important. Engineers, physicists, rocket scientists, philosophers and snake oil salesmen have all tried to share with us their opinions, their experiences or their 'secrets' to the perfect putt. In fact, one nuclear physicist at Edinburgh University has identified the easiest putt from the point of view of theoretical physics: it's the downhill putt, apparently. I have asked several pro golfers what they think of this, and they conclude that the nuclear physicist doesn't know anything about putting!

However, there is one basic truth which every teacher I have spoken to and every book I have read agrees upon when it comes to the actual act of making a putt: keep the body and head still throughout the stroke. Of course, there are other considerations: tempo, balance, follow-through, swing path and squareness of club face, to name but a few. But all of these are a matter of personal preference and secondary to the cardinal rule of putting – **keep the body and head still throughout the stroke.**

Let's study the average golfer on the green. Watch him carefully when he is standing over a putt: I am certain we will see body and head movement. Perhaps only a little, but some. Any movement takes our putt off the intended line. What we often attribute to a pushed or pulled short putt is actually caused by this movement, either by the body or the head. In fact the two are linked. Try moving your body and keeping your head completely still. It is impossible. It is marginally easier to keep the body still and move the head, but any movement in the head is automatically counterbalanced by the body.

The ideal position for putting is to hold the body absolutely still, almost like a statue. If someone tells us not to look out of the window or not to scratch our nose, this suddenly becomes the one thing we want to do. The same unconscious reaction happens when we tell ourselves not to move during our putting stroke. We try too hard. We become too rigid and consequently we introduce small movements which are not going to help. I have devised an exercise to help us create better balance. This exercise is very good for helping us stay aware of balance, but also useful in developing a consistently relaxed playing style.

STILLNESS ▶

You will need a full length mirror and your putter.

1. Stand in front of the mirror and assume your normal address position for putting, looking directly at yourself with your head up.

2. Ask someone to outline a box shape with white masking tape on the mirror around your head. They will need to leave a little gap between the tape and the top of your head, chin and ears.

3. Breathe in deeply a few times. Make sure there is no tension in your body. Pay particular attention to your shoulder muscles – this is where tension is most likely to manifest itself.

4. Once you feel relaxed and are breathing calmly, keep looking at yourself with your head contained within the tape box on the mirror. Make your putting stroke for a putt of about twelve feet.

5. Now notice any movement in your head. This is what we want to eliminate. Continue to make your putting stroke with a smooth tempo and pace until you can do it while keeping your head still. Concentrate on staying relaxed and keeping your head still.

A twelve-foot putt is a good length to imagine, because it needs a proper hit with the putter, but we can vary the distance for this exercise. This drill will for the first time not only give us an opportunity to see the movement of our heads, but will help us breathe and relax while preparing to putt.

When we know for sure we are able to stay balanced and still throughout the putting stroke, this bedrock of knowledge will remove doubt and prevent a loss of confidence. The knowledge that the basic platform from which we putt, balanced stillness, is in place is the foundation for building our confidence and developing a repeatable stroke on the green.

16

MEASURE AND REWARD

'Hard work beats talent when talent doesn't work hard.'

Anonymous

There is an old business maxim: what gets measured gets done, and what gets rewarded gets repeated.

Golf is a sport heavy on statistics. We can easily access statistics on every aspect of the game: driving distance, greens in regulation, sand saves, putts per green and putts per round. These figures can be very helpful. For amateurs, they give a real snapshot of what it takes to perform at the highest level. For the professionals, they provide a record against which they can measure improvement or decline. But very few amateur golfers keep any statistics at all. No doubt this is partly because we play golf for enjoyment, and generally we have a good sense of how we are playing compared to our 'normal' game. We tend to measure ourselves against our national handicap and whether we play to that on any round. Certainly few of us analyse our round in the way that a professional's round is analysed.

In order to **practise with purpose** we need to have goals when we step onto the practice putting green and we need to have a way of measuring our progress towards the realisation of those goals. Now, this may seem a little intense, especially for the average club golfer, but the only way we can know we are getting better is when our handicap comes down, and the only way to get our handicap down is to take fewer strokes per round. The place where we can reduce the number of strokes in the shortest period of time is on the green. Just think what a difference it would make if we could take three or four fewer putts per round.

I wonder what percentage of four-foot putts we sink? I doubt many of us know, to any degree of accuracy. And the reason is because we don't keep a record. But keeping records is easy. Many of us use devices on the course that give us distances, and many of them are capable of storing information that can later be downloaded.

Even if we don't want to keep a complete statistical record of our game, the one place where it is easy to keep tabs on our performance is on the practice putting green. We can record how many putts of a certain distance went in and how many did not. We can note how many putts we pushed, how many we pulled, how many long putts were short, or how many short putts were long. If we are serious about becoming a better putter, we need to have a standard against which we can compare ourselves. If we don't keep records, how can we know we're really improving over time?

I sometimes ask golfers after a round how they putted. Some will say, 'OK,' others will say, 'So, so,' and the rest will shrug their shoulders and grimace. If I then ask them how many putts they actually took, I doubt if one in a hundred could tell me. Obviously we know if we have putted well or badly, but precisely how well or how badly will be easier to assess if we have a number and not just a feeling.

When we keep statistical records of our practice sessions, the number becomes the goal. Let me explain what I mean. Imagine we take twelve balls to the green and set them up four feet from the hole as though they are the numbers on a clock face. We then proceed to play each of the putts and repeat this exercise. We will soon end up with an average number of successful putts. If we average six putts of twelve, we know we make fifty per cent of four-foot putts. If we then devise a practice routine to improve the quality of our four-foot putts, and raise that average from fifty to sixty per cent, this will save us one or two shots per round. It would also give us a target to improve upon: our practice would become more focused and more meaningful as a result.

Think about the concept of repeating what gets rewarded. I come from the carrot and not the stick school of motivation. Making ourselves sink a hundred consecutive putts before we are allowed to eat or go home, starting again from zero each time we miss, strikes me (for the average club golfer) as rather severe and difficult. Why not tell ourselves that if we sink those hundred consecutive short putts we can order our favourite meal, treat ourselves to a sports massage, or buy ourselves a dozen new golf balls? It's my belief that **we should associate success with pleasure and not punishment.**

The average golfer has a job in the real world, limited time to play and even less time to practise purposefully. So it is up to each individual to prioritise for themselves how important making serious improvement to their game really is. We all want to be better golfers, just as we all want to be more attractive, thinner, fitter, richer and happier – yet very few of us are truly willing to pay the price. If we are serious about making a step change in improving our putting, we need to make our practice more meaningful by keeping a record of our achievement, set goals to improve on those numbers, and reward ourselves when that improvement is achieved.

We are used to keeping a record of our other sporting achievements. At the gym we keep a record of the number of repetitions we can do on the various machines. We know the amount of weight we are able to push, and over a period of months we expect to see significant improvement.

When I spend summers in Edinburgh, I begin most mornings by hiking up a hill in the city centre called Arthur's Seat. The climb from the car park to the summit is 760 feet. Every time I go up, I use my stopwatch and try to beat my best time. If we can do this at the gym or when we're out walking, is it such a leap of the imagination to start keeping records of our putting statistics on the practice green?

Here are some exercises that will provide immediate statistical feedback against which we can set benchmarks of our current ability. These exercises will give a clear numerical target to improve upon.

FEEDBACK DRILL ▶

1. DISTANCE CONTROL

Take ten balls to the practice green and pick ten long-distance putts: over twenty feet in length. Putt the first ball to the first hole, the second to the second, and so on. When all ten balls have been played, walk up to each hole and make a note of how many balls are within three feet.

2. THREE-FOOTERS

Take ten balls and drop two balls each about three feet from five different holes. Using five different holes means that the putts demand different lines to the hole. This drill replicates the experience you will face on the course. Keep a record of how many of these three foot putts you make.

3. TWELVE-FOOTERS

This is similar to the previous drill. Take ten balls and drop two balls each about twelve feet away from five holes. Keep a record of how many you make and how many are within a foot.

4. THE PRO SIDE

When we miss a putt with a break on it, we tend to miss on the low side. This has also been known as the amateur side. Take ten balls and find a ten to twelve-foot putt, with at least twelve inches of break (the more the better). See how many you can either sink or miss on the high side.

EXERCISES *(continued)* ▶

5. DEAD STRAIGHT

Take ten balls and find a five-foot putt that is dead straight – no break whatsoever. Stand over this putt and imagine it is to win a major championship: really engage your imagination, sense the crowds, the commentators, the trophy. Create as much pressure as you can, then take the putt, and measure how many you make and how many you push or pull. This will help identify what your fault under pressure is going to be.

By keeping a record we will be able to see our improvement, which will translate into lower scores on the course. We should try to schedule proper practice at least once a week. **In the long term, the more we practise, the better we get.** We should also be sure to set rewards for ourselves as our putting stats improve.

PLAY

17

THE THREE Cs
(AND GETTING TO THE ZONE)

**'To my surprise, I found myself
making birdies.
I was in a calm mental state for
all of the 58 strokes.'**

Ryo Ishikawa, on shooting 58 on the Japan tour

It is early one balmy summer evening. We go out for a few holes, or maybe spend some time on the practice green, killing time with no real thoughts about what we are doing. Before we know it, putt after putt begins to fall. Those that don't drop hang on the edge. It is as though we have some mysterious power that is willing the ball into the hole on the perfect line. Have you ever experienced this scenario?

The thought dawns that we are 'in the zone'. There are no emotions, positive or negative, involved. How we got there, we do not know. How long we will remain there is anyone's guess. That it will come to an end is a certainty.

There are common characteristics of being in this state. The first, and most important, is **confidence**: a feeling of self-assurance, connected to positive self-esteem. The second is **full attention**, where the player is so fully in the moment that their attention is on the shot in hand to the exclusion of everything else, either physical (weather, background noise) or mental (negative thoughts or internal chatter). There is no separation between the player and the putt. Third there is a sense of **enjoyment**, whereby the process is pleasurable, and totally free from anxiety or fear, such is the level of calm. The fourth is **relaxation**, as the player feels no tension in their mind or body, and the final characteristic I have identified is **awareness**. This is not the same as full attention. It is a quality of mind which involves the player being fully connected to their surroundings, but not consciously influenced by or reactive to them. In this state they *know* what they need to do in relation to the world around them and have freed themselves to let it happen.

If we return to the memory of that early evening round or the fifteen aimless minutes spent on the putting green, how can all these factors suddenly have appeared in our game? Was it simply a random event? Or was there another trigger?

I have spent a long time contemplating my very best days on the green, comparing them to my very worst. The difference is now as clear as day: when I putted really well I allowed myself to putt without fear, to putt without any thought of the outcome. I putted like it just didn't matter. But when I tried to take that feeling into a competition or a match, I couldn't do it, because all of a sudden the putts *did* matter. This is the paradox we all face as golfers – **the more we try, the more we become physically aware and increase the risk of getting in our own way.**

Having studied a great deal of literature and thinking on peak performance during my career, I am convinced that while *understanding* how to get into the zone is worthwhile, it is ultimately unlikely to help us *perform* under pressure. It is my belief that the solution to this problem of 'getting in our own way' lies in practice – in adopting the mental and physical routines that embed the best habits of mind and body.

When faced with that pressure putt we cannot just stop, return to the practice green and work through our drills. There is no magical switch that will enable us to recover our previous form. But there is a simple mental approach that can help us on the green, and this is built around a concept call The Three Cs:

CONFIDENCE

We must believe we are good putters; we must believe we *can* make the putt. Maintaining this confidence is paramount, so we should never 'trash-talk' ourselves, never carry a bad putt forward. We need to think and speak well of ourselves as putters and players; to encourage ourselves, hold our heads high, build on our successes and learn from our mistakes.

COURAGE

We need to accept failure as a possible outcome, but not let that influence our putting routine and stroke. We need to be willing to miss and learn from missing, rather than be broken by it. Even when self-doubt whispers in our ears, we need the desire to try again, to hold our nerve and trust our line on a short must-make putt, never entertaining thoughts of self-doubt or fear.

COMMITMENT

When we prepare to putt, we commit to making the best stroke we can. When we entertain self-doubt, it is easy to pull or push a short, straight putt, as we try to steer the ball into the hole. Commit to the line, commit to the pre-shot routine and commit to the stroke.

If we care too much we try too hard. As I have mentioned before, too often we get in our own way and create unfavourable conditions for putting well. When we approach each putt with confidence, courage and commitment, there is nothing else to worry about. Then we really *can* putt to the best of our abilities.

18

IN PURSUIT OF
PUTTING EXCELLENCE

'When you go out onto the stage, all the preparation has to be forced into your subconscious. For the moment of the performance, we all have to return to a new level of unconsciousness. All the reflection and all the doubts have to be laid aside before you start.'

Dietrich Fischer-Dieskau

Meteorologists use the term 'perfect storm' to describe an event where a rare combination of circumstances occurs randomly but in a sequence that creates a storm of epic magnitude. If one of the contributing factors were not present, the storm would not occur with such force. Such events are rare, but their effects can be devastating. The expression 'perfect storm' is now used in popular culture as a description of a worst-case scenario.

We all have days on the golf course when everything comes together, and we are able to putt perfectly. On that day, with no thoughts or worries to impede it, our game becomes as easy and natural as walking up the fairway. On those magical days the hole is the size of a bucket. We do not think about our stroke, the position of our feet or hands or the length of our backswing. We read the line of the putt immediately and we trust our read. We roll putt after putt into the centre of the hole with dead weight.

Every golfer has a story of the day when everything went right. I had my moment in a match at Gaylord Golf Club in Michigan. On the first green I rolled in a five-foot putt for par. That set me up for the round, and after that I could not miss. I holed every single putt within ten feet that day. What was even more satisfying was the way I managed to find the centre of the cup every time. On that day my long putts were also extremely accurate: they either shaved the hole or stopped within inches. Later in the match my opponent, now convinced I couldn't miss, gave me a three-foot putt which I don't think I would have conceded to myself. It was and remains the best putting performance of my golfing life. I felt I had conquered putting.

The next day I played again. I returned to the course fully expecting to continue my streak, but the bubble had burst. The perfect putting conditions were no longer in effect. Something had changed – but what?

In the 2012 PGA Transitions Championship at Copperhead Golf Course in Palm Harbor, Florida, triple major winner Padraig Harrington grabbed the headlines with a ten-under-par opening round of 61. In this amazing round, Harrington took just twenty-two putts. On fourteen of the holes he only required one putt. When he reached the eighteenth green he was faced with a fifteen-foot putt for a birdie and the course record. The way he had been putting that day, a fifteen-foot putt was almost a gimme. In his post round interview he said, 'When it's your day, it's your day. I could've turned my back on the eighteenth and I would have holed out.'

On the following day, day two of the tournament, the spell was broken. Harrington shot a two-over-par 73. On the sixth hole he missed a twelve-inch putt. His touch on the green seemed to have disappeared. In his post-round interview this time he said, 'I didn't have those fifteen-footers where you are not worried about pace. I tended to either have short putts or long putts, and I was tentative on the long putts.'

What a difference a day makes. On day one Harrington's confidence was such that he felt he could succeed with his back to the ball, yet the following day he used the word 'tentative' about his putting. He was uncertain and cautious. I believe his second-day problems can only be explained as a subtle loss of confidence.

By any measure, Padraig Harrington is a magnificent golfer. His three majors attest to that. His dedication to practice is legendary, and his attention to detail on the range is precise. So here is a player with the right skill-set. Yet even someone as skilled as Harrington is unable to bring his impressive ability into effect *on demand*.

In the interview he gave after the astonishing first round, Harrington also said something very revealing: 'I've been playing nicely in practice. I shot a 64 on Wednesday. I've been like that for a long time now. I play better on Monday, Tuesday and Wednesday than I do on Thursday, Friday, Saturday and Sunday. I know my game is good. One of the hardest things is to wait for the confidence.'

Monday, Tuesday and Wednesday are the practice rounds, where the score does not count. The tournament starts on Thursday and then every shot counts. That introduces a very different pressure to each shot, and if there is one thing we know about pressure it is that it erodes confidence if we do not have a coping strategy to manage it.

After my perfect putting round I did not suffer a loss of confidence; in fact, the effect was quite the opposite. I expected to putt as I had done on that day. I felt as if I had mastered putting (obviously I'd had too much sun the day before). However, that expectation unwittingly created pressure for me. It made me more self-conscious of what I was doing and much less intuitive. I started to try too hard on the greens. If I had a poor putt early in the round, it dented my confidence. I did what we all do. I allowed it to bother me, and of course more poor putts quickly followed.

We should putt with a positive expectation, but we should not be attached to the outcome. The ball is either going to go in or not, but it is important to retain some detachment, take that outcome in our stride and get on with the game.

When I first started watching golf on television I used to wonder why the television companies concentrated so much on what was happening on the green. I wanted to see big, booming drives or majestic irons, not short, seemingly simple putts! I quickly realised that the putting green is generally where tournaments are won and lost; it's where the golfer shows their mettle. Like Ben Hogan in the mid-1950s, it's no use being the best tee-to-green player in the world if we are unable to sink putts.

I am sure you have heard the old saying, 'You drive for show; you putt for dough.' I first heard this when I was a wee boy back in the early 1960s. So if putting is so important, what makes the perfect putter?

I suppose you could define the 'perfect putter' as someone who only takes eighteen putts in a round of golf – one putt on every green. Since 1979, in PGA tour events, there have been seven players, including Corey Pavin, who have attained the impressive landmark of taking eighteen putts in a single round. Incredibly, in the second round of the 2002 Air Canada Championship, Stan Utley took only six putts in the first nine holes.

Such feats are rare, however, and inevitably apply to those extraordinary days when a player is on a streak and feels they can't miss. What we are looking for in our own game is consistency: a stroke which we can rely on day in, day out. The statistic I found most impressive when researching putting records was that in 2008 Tiger Woods did not miss a single putt from inside five feet in tournament play. We can immediately see that a golfer with that kind of consistency will have huge faith in their putting.

On 29 September Luke Johnson three-putted the sixteenth hole of his opening round of a tournament. Nothing unusual about that, perhaps – except that it was the first three-putt he had made in the previous 449 holes of tournament play. In an age of obsessive golfing stats, Johnson's run of 449 consecutive holes without a three-putt is the greatest recorded putting streak of all time. Imagine how confident he felt on the green!

When I worked in television I was once involved in producing a magic series for Saturday evenings. One of the show's regular features involved a guest magician from America. They were generally close-up magicians whose tricks involved very few props other than ropes, cards or other small items. They performed with consummate ease and professionalism.

Part of the contract for appearing on the show was a first-class return air fare to London and four nights in a hotel. Inevitably, some of the magicians would want to stay longer, but couldn't afford the cost of the hotels. As I had just bought my first apartment and had an extra bedroom, I always offered the visiting magician the use of my spare room. In return, they had to teach me a coin or card trick.

The tricks were always of a technical nature: they required a degree of dexterity, while at the same time appearing to be easy and natural. I was a good learner, but even with a world-class magician giving me one-to-one tuition, I could not master any of the moves in such a short time. I always asked my guest how long it had taken them to master the trick and the answer was always the same: 'Years.'

They told me stories of thousands of hours spent as children, alone in their bedrooms, learning the moves, then practising them over and over and over again. These were some of the greatest magicians in the world, and I saw, without exception, that their true 'secret' was that they practised relentlessly – and in so doing raised the level of their skill to pure brilliance. Many other magicians might know how the tricks were done, but they were unable to execute them because they had not invested the time to master the skills required.

The lesson of the magicians was not lost on me: **excellence in any endeavour is the result of practice** and not good fortune.

19

INTERESTING STATS

**'You don't always get what you wish for;
you get what you work for.'**

Anonymous

On the professional tour there are detailed records of players' putting averages. One of the most revealing sets of statistics shows that players with the lowest average putts per round are most frequently in the money on Sunday afternoon. It is no coincidence that the top putters on the PGA tour are among the top players in the world rankings.

In 2012 the best putter on the USPGA tour was Zach Johnson. Over 51 rounds Johnson had an average of 27.80 putts per round. To put the quality of putting on the whole tour into perspective, we should notice that the lowest-ranked player, Scott Stallings (184th), maintained an average of 30.25 putts per round: this shows how well a golfer needs to putt to make it at all as a professional.

It is difficult to make comparisons between professional golfers and amateurs because we do not have the statistics about ourselves, but examining the numbers of the best golfers in the world can give us a realistic view of what to expect from ourselves. It is clear that anyone who can get their putting average down to thirty or less will start to post a very low score indeed, but we are not professional golfers and are not dedicated to relentless practice or imitation of the skills and of these great players. Such a target may be a little ambitious for most of us, then, but any reduction in our putting average will lead to a more positive attitude and, of course, lower scores.

The different lengths of putts pros face on the tour can make the difference between winning and losing, and in the amateur game we face the same challenges. Knowing what the putting statistics mean will prevent us humble amateurs being too hard on ourselves. According to the statistics from the US and European tours, pros on average make 90 per cent of three-foot putts, 65 per cent of five-foot putts and 20 per cent of ten-foot putts. From twenty feet, tour pros only make two to three per cent of putts.

The data don't record percentages of putts sunk from over twenty feet, but there is another, very revealing number. Professionals get an astonishing 85 per cent of lag putts from twenty feet or more to within three feet of the hole. We can see why pros don't expect to take more than two putts on a hole. This last piece of information shows why we need to get more of those longer putts up to the hole: doing so will give us a better chance of only taking two putts on the hole.

However, the most important message I take from all this data is that we should not to be so hard on ourselves. If, on average, a pro fails to make 35 per cent of five-foot putts, we certainly shouldn't be too dejected when we, mere amateurs, perform less impressively than this. Let's embrace these realities and let them relax us!

THINK OF 1000 PUTTS

Imagine keeping track of a thousand putts over a number of rounds. I would be curious to know what percentage of our putts we think would fall into the following categories:

a) Perfect
b) Good
c) Acceptable
d) Poor
e) Awful

I have worked through this exercise with golfers who complain about their putting. When I do so, I first ask them what percentage of their putts they think fall into category five: *awful*. On average their answer to this question is usually 15 per cent or less. Then the number of putts they class as *poor* is about 10 per cent. When I point out that this means they think 75 per cent of the putts they take are *acceptable, good* or *perfect*, the response is usually a wry smile and a shake of the head.

Most golfers tell me that it is the poor and awful shots that are causing them the most grief, and it is those that they want to eradicate. While I am sympathetic to their desire and share it as well, I simply want to draw their attention to how they *feel* about themselves as a putter. I know very few club golfers who would describe themselves as 'great' putters. In my experience, most club golfers say they are good, average or poor. These are the same putters who tell me that 75 per cent of the putts they take are acceptable or better! In my book that's good putting. Obviously good is not the same as brilliant, wonderful or perfect, but 'good' is a great place from which to start.

To build our confidence on the greens we need to believe we are good putters. If we simply focus on our bad putts – the 25 per cent we think are poor or awful – we erode our confidence as putters. **A loss of confidence leads to an inner expectation that we will hit bad putts and miss easy ones.** This inner expectation in turn forms the subconscious self-image of ourselves as poor putters, and the more we consciously reinforce this notion of ourselves, the deeper we imprint it within the mind. This results not only in our performing in accordance with our subconscious self-image; the poor performance reinforces the belief that is its underlying cause.

I have met a few golfers who in their early careers were brilliant players with representative honours and what seemed to be a sparkling career ahead of them. But in many instances these anticipated careers were never realised because, impressive as their game was, the sad reality was that when it mattered they just couldn't putt. How often have you heard someone referred to as 'a player who would be on the tour if only they could putt'? Too often, I am sure. I believe it is a mental block, an internal subconscious 'yip' that makes them focus on the pain rather than the pleasure of the game.

The following is a simple confidence-building drill that I use with players. Often we are too hard on ourselves; this exercise helps to combat that impulse.

ACCENTUATE THE POSITIVE ▶

1. Go to the practice green with as many balls as there are holes on the putting green.
2. Line the balls up in a row.
3. Putt one ball to each of the holes on the putting green. Take as long as you want over each putt. Pace it out, look at it from all sides, go through the routine, take a few practice strokes. In fact, do what you do on the course in competition. Or simply putt them one after the other without too much time in between.
4. Once you have taken the stroke, watch it and decide if it was good, acceptable or poor. You will find that the majority (75 per cent or more of the putts) are 'good' or 'acceptable', and only a few putts will be poor.

The aim of this exercise is to **encourage a positive mind-set when assessing our putting**. It will help us avoid judging ourselves in a negative way. Ideally, we should think of ourselves as good putters;

one of the best ways to do this is to **stop being too harsh on ourselves**. It is a destructive habit that we lapse into when we simply focus on the poor putts instead of those we think of as being in the range of acceptable to good.

Another way of approaching this idea is to imagine ourselves coaching a young player who is new to the game – someone keen to learn and who wants to improve. The young player has asked us to help him become a better putter. When we join him on the practice green, how do we speak to this golfer? What feelings about himself would we want the young player to end the session with? If he hits poor putts would we seek to encourage him with constructive suggestions or would we roll our eyes and tell him his putting was poor?

I think we would encourage him. We would seek to extract and accentuate all the positive aspects from the shots we watched him play – and to help him learn from those that didn't go so well. So we should put ourselves in that same position during our own putting: **we should treat ourselves as our own coach**, be kind to ourselves, be positive and encouraging. Above all, we need to stop being so hard on ourselves.

Only a tiny fraction of the people on this planet who play golf actually make a full-time living from it – even within the professional ranks. Fewer still get rich! **Comparing ourselves to a professional player is not a helpful process.** Rather what we should do is compare ourselves with ourselves: keep a record of the number of putts we make per round, then recall and determine what percentage of the putts was in our opinion poor, compared with those that were good or acceptable.

We then set ourselves a target of increasing the good putts. It may seem obvious, but what this does is very important. It gives us, both consciously and unconsciously, a clear goal. It gives us a point of reference to measure our improvement or decline. This feedback is very helpful and is something very few handicap golfers use.

20

THINK INSTINCTIVELY ON THE LONG PUTTS

'Instinct is untaught ability.'

Alexander Bain

Have you ever screwed up a piece of paper and thrown it into a waste basket? We've all thrown a ball of paper or a plastic bottle into a bin over fifteen feet away and been pleasantly surprised when it landed directly in without touching the sides. More often than not it was an instinctive throw; we did not take practice throws or ask advice on the exact distance. On these occasions we just looked and then threw.

If we hit the basket first time, the next throw will be a little more challenging. This is not because it's different, but because we are no longer relying on intuition and instinct to guide us. Instead we are engaged in distance analysis or thinking about our technique – concerns which first time round we had not considered. We may even be taking some practice throws to get a feel for the point at which we should release the item from our hands. We have gone from unconscious to conscious action.

When we take a first look at a long putt we get an instinctive 'first read' of the line and pace required for the shot. I have found, just like the quickly taken throw into a waste basket, that the more we can trust our first read and feel on the longer putts, the closer we're likely to get the ball. Otherwise we start over-thinking and become too mechanical.

From the previous chapter we can see the importance of getting the long putts close to increase the probability of making the next one.

Distance control on the green is obviously a long way from throwing rubbish into a waste basket. One is played in the air and the other on the ground. The speed of the greens is an ever-changing factor, due to the length of the grass, contours on the green, direction of the grain and sometimes the wind. Even a powerful computer would struggle to model all these factors and calculate the correct line and pace for any given putt. Yet our capacity to make the same assessment mentally is incredibly sophisticated. And it is best done without over-thinking. Rather we should trust our innate ability to see a target and instantly determine the required technique and touch.

This ability to execute a seemingly complex mental calculation and adapt our actions instantaneously is seen in many sports: a quarterback throwing an exact distance to a moving target, often while in motion himself; a tennis player playing a delicate angled volley after arriving at the ball at great speed; a cricketer running out an opposing batsman while off balance and with only one stump to aim at. How much time do any of these athletes have to think through their actions? Very little indeed. Often the throw or volley comes down to pure feel and instinct. Yet in golf we seemingly have all the time in the world to think about our long putts, to walk around the green, take multiple practice strokes and try to calculate exactly how hard we need to hit the ball and along which line.

When approaching long putts, we know the statistical probability of the ball going into the hole is low. So **we should play the percentage shot and get the ball into the three-foot zone.** Now this is no revelation: this lagging of the putt as close to the hole as possible is something we learn from very early in our golfing education. Nevertheless, **long-distance control is an aspect of the game that gets too little attention on the practice green**, and generally on very long-distance putts we have a tendency to hit without too much expectation and hope for the best.

In putting, golf differs from most other ball sports, as the shot travels over the ground, and the speed of the green, along with the contours, adds variables which change with every stroke. The quarterback or tennis player knows that the resistance of the air is constant, and the throw or shot will generally follow a straight line. So by its nature the perfect putt involves a more complicated calculation. This is why we need to trust our first, instinctive 'read' in terms of pace and line.

The following exercise is designed to help us become more instinctive on long putts. If possible, it is best completed on a course green rather than the practice green. This is because we can soon learn the breaks and nuances on our practice greens, and though we can replicate most of the putts we will experience, we cannot recreate actual playing conditions. I do this exercise if I am playing alone and the course is quiet. You will need one ball.

SENSE THE DISTANCE ▶

1. Throw the ball a long way from the hole.
2. Once the ball has come to rest, walk up to it as you would during a real round, and mark it.
3. Look at the putt from behind the ball only, and simply trust the read of the break you decide upon.
4. Place the ball back in position, address the ball and look down the line of the putt.
5. Do not make a practice stroke. Just sense how firmly the putt needs to be played.
6. See in your mind the ball taking the line you have chosen and coming to settle within three feet of the hole.
7. Take the putt.

The purpose of this exercise is to become used to seeing a new putt for the first time, as we would out on the course. Being on an actual green makes the whole experience more realistic. We can indulge our imagination: 'Two putts for the Open Championship'; 'Two putts to win the Ryder Cup.' We should make the putt feel important and real, and learn to trust our gut feel and not over-think or become overly mechanical.

If we are relaxed and instinctive when we throw the paper at the waste basket, we are more likely to make it than if we are tense and uncertain. We need to remember this when we size up the lag putts.

21

EXPECT TO MAKE IT

'The better you putt, the bolder you play.'

Don January

I really enjoy any putt up to six inches in length. In fact such putts are just perfect, because I have never missed one in my life. When I step up to knock one in, I do so in the certain knowledge that I have never missed one, and will not miss this one either. I am absolutely 100 per cent sure it's going in.

Imagine having that same feeling over every putt; imagine the relaxed uninhibited stroke free from any tension or sense of trying. It would be an ideal state. We know it's impossible to sink every putt, but it is possible to take every putt with a sense of assured confidence that 'we can make the putt'. In other words, we are capable of making a good stroke free from any negative thoughts or unwanted nervousness.

On the putting green we are aware that **self-doubt is unhelpful at best and damaging at worst**. There is no evidence I can find to suggest that being nervous, angry, tense or negative makes us better putters. None at all. So why bother with it? Why do we get so hung up emotionally over putts which even on a practice green we would not expect to sink every time?

It is human nature to want to succeed and win: when we do so we feel good, and when we fail we feel disappointed or frustrated, or think of ourselves as failures. This is why so few players smile after a missed putt! Obviously there's nothing to smile about, and our natural emotional response to failure is distress. However, **negative self-talk and self-doubt are created by our minds and not the green**; we have the ability to read the putt and make an informed choice as to the line. **If we trust our first read and feel for the strength of the putt, we are more likely to make a positive stroke.** If we doubt our read and are unsure of the pace, it will be impossible to make a tension-free stroke.

Trusting our first read is hard because our ego gets in the way. We don't want to display a 'couldn't care less' attitude after a cursory glance at the ball; we don't want to look like we're thinking, 'Maybe it will go in; maybe it won't.' I am convinced, however, that most players would be more mentally and physically at ease if they did.

I make this claim based on my belief that **there is no perfect way to putt, but there is a *best way for each of us*.** This best way will feel natural and comfortable, and once we find it we should trust it. Sadly, few golfers ever truly trust their stroke; they are forever tinkering with it and seeking advice. Even the great Seve Ballesteros, who was one of the best putters on the European and PGA tour for a long time, was seen on the putting green before tournaments, inviting other players to take a look at his stroke. In fact, most pros are searching for the 'missing piece' of their stroke, as though there is something wrong with it. The great majority of the time it's probably all in their head. As we've seen, one of the greatest putters in the history of the game, Bobby Jones, had an awkward-looking, unconventional stroke, that by today's standards would be ridiculed, yet he holed more clutch putts than any other player in his era. His stance, swing path and follow-through went against conventional wisdom. But his trust in his stroke was unshakeable.

For the average golfer, unless we have a repeating fault that requires a diagnosis from an experienced pair of eyes, we will generally figure out the solution for ourselves: the best putting owes more to feel than mechanical technique. Although we should never hesitate to consult a professional or take a putting lesson if self-improvement proves elusive, provided we are willing to invest the time to work through our challenges on the green and then set about fixing them, I believe we will eventually find our instinctive 'feel'. We're all familiar with those days on the course when our touch deserts us. We say, 'I just don't know why I am leaving everything short . . . pulling every putt . . . pushing every putt . . . charging everything past the hole.' Invariably this happens because of self-doubt and low expectations. When we are afflicted by self-doubt, even the shortest putts seem missable.

The next time we experience a loss of touch on the course, we should not despair; rather, we should recognise that we are now in the ideal space to **putt without any concern for the outcome**. After all, things couldn't get any worse, could they?

When we take a putt there are only two possible outcomes: it goes in or it doesn't. When the ball drops, that's perfect; when it doesn't, we shouldn't berate ourselves, as to do so is the fastest way to erode our confidence.

This lack of confidence is not necessarily something we're aware of. Often it's something that begins to work its way into our thinking after the first poor putt. If these negative thoughts at a subconscious level are responsible for the self-doubt, then we must ask who put them there in the first place? The answer is simple: we did.

Child psychologists estimate that 96 per cent of four-year-old children have high self-esteem and high levels of confidence. This is due to their parents and close family heaping positive affirmations, praise and unconditional love on them. Their self-image at this age is at an all-time high. Yet by the age of eighteen, less than three per cent of these young people will still have high self-esteem and self-confidence. Why? When a child goes to school at the age of around four or five, they suddenly get exposed to rival, often 'negative', views of themselves. From innocuous schoolyard name-calling to teachers and other adults giving them deliberate or unintentional criticism, telling them they're lazy, stupid, naughty or clumsy, children are suddenly exposed to comments that undermine their positive self-image. The child grows up to think of themselves as lazy, stupid or clumsy because, at a subconscious level, that is what they have been taught to believe.

Every golfer's mind contains a self-image that is linked to and informs their performance expectations when they are on the course. If they have spent years being negative or nursing low expectations, that is what their subconscious mind will find when it looks for memories of past experiences.

We can change that by changing our thoughts and attitudes about ourselves and our expectations. Better to expect to make a putt and be surprised when it does not drop, than to expect to miss a putt and feel validated in our expectation when it misses. This is as simple as making a determined commitment to take a positive view of ourselves on the greens and not get annoyed or upset with ourselves when we miss.

22

NEVER PUTT THE GIMME

'Your self-confidence must be maintained.'

Christy Mathewson

We've all been given putts in match-play. Sometimes our opponent concedes because they believe we can't possibly miss, or perhaps it's a friendly match and they don't want to start with an overly competitive attitude. In competition, however, the gimme may be tactical: conceding the easy short putts early in the game, with a view to making us play a short one later in the round, when the pressure is on.

The tactics of match-play are as diverse as the personality types who play; therefore it is important to expect to have to hole every putt. I have seen players give a lot of short putts to their opponent in the front nine, and then on the back nine give nothing at all, even twelve-inch putts. A player begins expecting to be given the putt and then becomes annoyed when they're made to play; this irritation infects their game, making them frustrated and tense. In this situation, all of a sudden the next two-footer looks anything but easy.

Whenever I am given a putt, I pick up my ball. I have noticed other players accept the given putt, but then go ahead and take it anyway. This is not against the rules of golf and, one may argue, neither is it against the etiquette or spirit of match-play, but to go ahead and take the putt we've just been given is, in my opinion, a mistake. I prefer to imagine, without any doubt at all, that I would have made the putt.

If I saw the gimme as an opportunity to putt without any consequences and then missed, how would I feel? More importantly, what would my opponent learn from it? My confidence would certainly take a knock, and I would have needlessly introduced doubt to my mind. By accepting the gimme and picking up the ball, I remain positive and confident.

To win – or at least play our best – **we must keep ourselves in the most positive state of mind possible on the green**, and this means avoiding situations where that feeling could be damaged. To risk missing a short putt we need not take seems to me a poor choice. Why not take a few practice strokes without a ball instead? Then the given putt is one we believe without any doubt we would have made.

We have all experienced that relief when we're given a short putt by our opponents. But we need to acknowledge the negative thoughts we were entertaining ('I didn't like the look of that') and eliminate any self-doubt; we need to stand over every short putt with the full belief that we will make it. **In match-play, we must not rely on the benevolence of our opponent; that's not a strategy, that's wishful thinking.**

In the Open Championship played at Turnberry in 1977 Jack Nicklaus and Tom Watson were playing together for the final thirty-six holes in what became known as the 'Duel in the Sun'. The two greatest golfers on the planet went head to head, each getting better and better in the final round. In stroke-play competition there are no gimmes; all balls must be holed out. But the mind-set and factors which cause us to lose confidence are much the same.

The 1977 Open came down to the last hole, with Watson one stroke ahead. Off the tee he found the middle of the fairway, and Nicklaus, in an attempt to hit a huge drive, pushed his ball right, into light rough close to gorse bushes. Watson played a now famous seven-iron to twenty inches from the hole, and his caddy told him he was going to win the Open. Watson had seen enough to know this was far from certain, and sure enough, from the deep rough, Nicklaus powered an iron onto the front of the green, some forty feet from the hole.

As the pair walked to the green with the fans stampeding behind them, Watson turned to his caddy, Alfie Fyles, and said, 'He's going to make that putt.' Watson steeled himself for the fact that he would have to make his own putt to win. He prepared himself mentally for Nicklaus making the forty-footer, so it would not be a shock to him when it happened. And he was right to do so.

Dramatically, Nicklaus made the putt for an amazing birdie on the seventy-second hole. Yet Watson was not intimidated; after Nicklaus had sunk this monster birdie putt, Watson wasted no time in stepping up and replacing his ball. He steadied himself over his own putt, and stroked it dead centre into the hole.

KNOCK IT IN ▶

Here is a simple exercise we can incorporate into our practice to help us become more willing to go with our instincts and stop trying to over-control our stroke on short putts. It requires three balls, any iron we wish and our normal putter.

1. On the practice putting green select a three-foot putt. Place the three balls on the ground; take the iron you selected.

KNOCK IT IN *(continued)* ▶

2. Don't take long reading the line of the putt, but be sure to pick a line you trust. Then as quickly as you are comfortable with, putt the three balls to the hole. (Decide for yourself how you want to strike the ball with the iron – with the flange, using the loft or even left-handed; it doesn't matter as this exercise is about instinct and feel, not mechanics.) The important thing is to focus on making the putt, not the fact you have the wrong club.
3. Now move to a different three-foot putt and repeat the drill, this time with your usual putter.
4. Repeat this drill at least twice and see how many balls you holed with the iron versus the putter.

We find with this exercise that sometimes there is little difference between the iron and the putter, and that concentrating on simply trying to make the putt and adapting to the incorrect club enables us to putt with lower expectations. The purpose of the exercise is to demonstrate that when we trust our read and relax (which with an iron as a putter is all we can do), our sense of feel will allow us to make more good putts than we might have expected.

As important as it is that we love our putter, we must equally have faith in our stroke. Irrespective of how perfect the putter feels, if our stroke lacks authority or conviction, a good putt becomes impossible. When we use an iron our expectations will naturally be low, and paradoxically we will be more instinctive in how we strike the ball.

We must be prepared to make every short putt, and to do this we need to focus on our own task, not what our partner may or may not do. Watson's mental approach on the final green of the 1977 Open Championship was perfect. He did not get ahead of himself. He did not rely on Nicklaus missing to give him two putts from twenty inches to win. Had he not prepared himself mentally, who knows how he would have felt over that putt?

From three feet there is only one strategy: sink the putt. The more we treat it as routine – just reading it and trusting our ability to make it – the better prepared we will be mentally to do so. Anything with the potential to undermine this self-trust, - such as missing a putt we have just been given, should be avoided.

23

READY, STEADY, GO

**'We are what we repeatedly do.
Excellence therefore,
is not an act but a habit.'**

Aristotle

I remember from my schooldays that races were almost always begun with the words, 'Ready . . . Steady . . . Go!' As I reflect on the challenges of the putting green, I realise that **many golfers putt without being ready**. They are in a hurry to get the putt over with, resigned to the fact it's probably not going to go in. These players believe they have learned through hard experience that preparation isn't going to make a bit of difference. Their level of concentration is generally poor, they don't take their read properly and, other than a practice stroke (or not), they just step up and play the shot. If this works for you, fine – but for most players it won't. We have to be *ready*.

READY

We should never take a putt before we're ready. Professionals on tour take as much time as they need to prepare for the putt. Before taking the stroke, we need to prepare in our minds the nature of the putt we are about to take. Have we read the putt and taken into consideration the factors that will influence it? The amount of break, uphill or downhill, whether it follows the grain or goes into the grain, the speed of the green, or any other factors that need to be taken into account. Until we've considered the variables it would be poor judgement to go ahead and set up to take the stroke.

For too many golfers the 'getting ready' phase is different every time they play. Sometimes they take their time, other times they seem to be in such a hurry. For me, **the 'getting ready' phase is more mental than physical: we need to be as quiet mentally as possible**. The 'getting ready' phase is the part of the putting routine where we are absorbing information – it is thinking time.

However, there is no need to prolong this stage of our pre-shot preparation – to make it overly conscious. Our brains process information instantly, so the read is generally quick. Whether we trust that read is another matter.

When I have played with a caddy, they have sometimes told me something that I don't see or agree with. As they are the local and know the course, I will usually trust their read. However, if they are wrong, I will have less faith in their read next time; I will be less relaxed before the putt. At that point I have to decide either to go with the caddy's reads or not. I will listen to them but ultimately decide on the line for myself.

Many tour events are played at world-class golf courses where there are full-time regular caddies available. Yet the professionals work with their own caddies, and figure out the greens after a few practice rounds and some discussion. This suggests that the art of reading the green is a skill, and, as with all skills, we should always be seeking to develop and improve it.

STEADY

Once we have gone through our pre-shot analysis and routine, picked our line and decided on the pace, we are ready. Next we need to steady ourselves, or 'get set'. This is when we take our stance over the ball, and **settle into a relaxed physical and mental state, free from self-doubt, anxiety or tension in our shoulders or arms.** Just like a sprinter, or any other athlete who begins from a stationary position, to make the best possible putt we need to be in our 'right' body position. This is the stance we feel most comfortable with. Once there, we are, in a sense, in the blocks, raised and ready for the gun to fire.

GO

After our preparation, we simply 'go': we begin the stroke. Our 'go' is a trigger we use to initiate the stroke. Many golfers use a forward press of their hands, but any physical motion can serve as a trigger to initiate the stroke.

Breaking our putting system into simple repeatable actions helps develop a consistent routine – a tried and trusted sequence that means there's one less thing to think about when we are under pressure.

As simple as it sounds, the notion of Ready Steady Go will stop us putting when we are not ready. It is especially helpful when we hit a short one as far past the hole as the original putt and have to play again. Even at the highest level, when a short putt is missed the player invariably rushes the next stroke. They may be angry with the poor stroke and want to get off the green as quickly as possible; it is a natural response. But if we give in to this kind of emotional hijacking and fail to prepare for the return putt, the odds are that we will not be in the right state of mind to play the next shot to the best of our ability.

24

READ IT, TRUST IT, PUTT IT

**'If your train's on the wrong track,
every station you come to is the wrong station.'**

Bernard Malamud

Reading the line of a putt is part art and part skill. Some players seem to give the line little more than a cursory glance, while others incorporate their own particular ritual prior to setting up to take the stroke. They may get down low, look at it from two sides, check the grain of the grass, pace the distance to the hole, using all the various inputs to help them compute, then decide on the line.

As with all aspects of putting, **we need to find the most comfortable and successful way for ourselves**. Almost all golfers stand behind the ball and look down the line, and generally getting down low gives a better view of the contours and breaks. My view is that the first read will be good and in most circumstances should be trusted. When we are under pressure, doubts can creep in, so we look again and frequently start to over-analyse the breaks, and, rather than trust our first instincts, we begin seeing things which may not be there. This leads to confusion, and this **uncertainty is the last thing we need when we are about to putt.**

Once we have read the putt and picked our line, we should not doubt it. Doubt will move us from a state of unconscious excellence to conscious self-awareness, where the very act of trying to control the swing or the stroke will make us tighten up and putt without conviction or authority.

From personal experience I believe that most of the time we get a very good sense of the right line, and only occasionally do we misread it. This means that the majority of our putts, if hit on the right line, have a good chance of going in. When I speak with players who are having problems on the green, it is often their unwillingness to trust their read or their stroke that lies at the heart of their poor performance. From experience, I know that just **telling people to relax and trust themselves on the course rarely helps**; instead I advise them to **experiment with feel on the practice green and not to be too fixated on mechanics**.

THE TOURNAMENT CHALLENGE ▶

Here is a simple exercise to incorporate during a practice round on the golf course. It will help us become more willing to trust our instincts and stop trying to over-control the stroke. I recommend trying this exercise on the course rather than the practice green (as long as no one's waiting behind you), as over time we get to know the breaks and nuances of the practice green. After a few long putts we get a good sense of the pace of the green, which is not possible on the first green of a new course.

1. Stand at the flag and throw the ball to the furthest point on the green from the flag.
2. When the ball has come to rest, walk up to it as you would normally and mark it.
3. Imagine you are on the final hole of a major tournament, and the green is surrounded by grandstands. You need to get down in two putts to win.
4. Take a look at the line and pace of the putt, and trust it. No second-guessing.
5. Go through your pre-putt routine, then take the putt.

THE TOURNAMENT CHALLENGE *(continued)* ▶

6. Wherever it comes to rest, you now have to make that putt for glory. Trust your first read, and play the line and pace you see.

7. Pay attention to how close to the hole the first read goes.

The purposes of this exercise are to get us used to trusting our first instincts regarding direction and pace, and to avoid second-guessing ourselves when under pressure.

The more we do this, the more we will realise that our innate sense of distance, feel and pace is better than we had hitherto given ourselves credit for. We will learn to have more trust in our instincts.

25

NEVER UP, NEVER IN

'I'm a great believer that if you don't get the ball to the hole, it won't go in.'

Colin Montgomerie

Some quotations are so well worn they have become clichés: 'You can't teach an old dog new tricks', 'You can lead a horse to water but you can't make it drink', 'The early bird gets the worm.' We have heard them so often that we no longer really listen, let alone consider the wisdom they might contain.

Golf too has its various clichés, but in putting there is one that stands above all others: 'Never up, never in.' Chances are this phrase is uttered at some point on every course in every country every day! If a putt does not reach the hole, clearly there are no circumstances under which it can go in. A putt coming up short, especially on the right line, is always frustrating, as we recognise we have done the hard part, got the read perfectly and sent the ball down the right line – we just haven't given it enough juice.

Coming up short can happen on a putt of any length. However, it is probably more common on longer putts, where players are worried about hitting it too hard and going a long way past the hole. The result is a tentative stroke that leaves the ball well short. Again, doubt is the crucial factor.

When a golfer is having trouble getting his longer putts up to the hole, there is a very simple drill I recommend, which proves it is not their distance perception that is the problem but their willingness to trust their feel. The drill goes like this: put the putter down, and then roll the ball by hand towards the hole. That's it. Curiously, golfers who do this find that more often than not when they roll the ball it gets a lot closer to the hole than when they putt from the same position.

The reasons for this, I believe, are twofold: first, without the putter in hand we are guided more by intuition than by process – we don't over-think the distance; and second, because we know that rolling the ball along the ground is not a golf shot, our expectation is low, so we relax and roll the ball more instinctively. Free from anxiety, and no longer over-scrutinising the force required – we get it right.

When we hit any putt with the right amount of pace, there are two possible outcomes: the ball either goes into the hole or it misses it. A putt that comes up short of the hole only has one possible outcome: a miss. Putts which go past the hole have a better statistical chance of dropping into the hole. So, as clichéd as it may sound, 'never up, never in' is true. **To give ourselves a chance of making the putt we need to putt with conviction that we will get to the hole.**

I once played a thirty-six hole foursome match at Muirfield in Scotland and enjoyed the service of an excellent caddy who played off a handicap of three. On the first green he told me the greens were slow, as there had been a lot of rain, and to be sure to get the ball up to the hole. Consequently I knocked a six-foot putt for a par (and a win) four feet past the hole and gave my partner a character-building putt for the half. On the next green the caddy reminded me the greens were slow. But after my rush of blood on the first, I left my thirty-foot putt fifteen feet short; my partner missed the (easy) fifteen-footer I had left him for the half. By the time I came to the third green, I had no confidence in my judgement and feel for the pace of the greens, and had no clear sense of how hard I needed to putt the ball to get it close. The previously enthusiastic caddy gave me my putter and wearily reminded me to 'hit it firmly' to get it close.

Herein lies the challenge we all face when we lack feel or confidence: exactly how hard is 'hit it firmly'? It is very difficult to create a scale of force for putts, as this is subjective. I have been guilty over the years of encouraging a partner with well-intentioned but inappropriate words of wisdom before the stroke: 'Don't leave it short.' This kind of comment reminds me of the theatre director who watched an actor rehearse a scene, then, when the actor asked for some notes, thought for a while and scratched his chin before saying, 'The next time you play that scene, do it better.'

We need a better way to find the right pace and get the ball past the hole than simply telling ourselves to 'do it better'. **We need to trust our instinct and stroke the ball with our intuitive feel.** When I found myself with no feel as a consequence of those early putts at Muirfield, it was my confidence that had deserted me, not my ability. But on the day in question I no longer trusted my ability – I became more and more 'mechanical'. I looked for an escape route in the knowledge that things couldn't get any worse. My solution was to accept that the current approach wasn't working and that if I was going to putt badly, then better I putt badly with confidence and trust my instinct. I kept this up for the rest of the round and over the next few holes I started to find my range, discovering that sometimes the simple act of letting go of the consequences of a shot frees us from being inhibited when we play it.

The following exercises and suggestions can help us develop a more pro-active approach to regaining feel on the greens:

STRIKE WITH CONVICTION ▶

1. Remind yourself that if your putts come up short, the ball has no chance of going in.

2. On the practice green, take six balls and putt to six different holes of varying lengths. Make sure every ball goes past the hole. Don't worry how far past they go at first; simply focus on striking the ball with conviction.

3. If your putts are coming up short during a game, irrespective of your normal routine, make this one change: before any putt, step slightly back from your ball, look at the hole, and then, while looking at the hole, take three practice putts, visualising the ball rolling into the hole.

4. Be willing to run putts well past the hole rather than well short of the hole. If you run well past the hole it will be easier to throttle back on the next hole than to throttle up.

5. If you are just not getting up to the hole and cannot bring yourself to hit the ball firmly enough, do not succumb to the temptation to beat yourself up, or berate yourself for being a bad golfer. Exasperation can lead to distress and anxiousness, so stay focused on getting the line right, and always seek *something* positive from every negative experience.

A short putt is usually the result of being tentative and fearful of running the ball past the hole, leaving ourselves a trickier return putt. **Don't ever worry about the next putt; you may not have one.** Focus on the putt in hand. And remember, **better too long than too short**.

26

STILL THE MIND
OVER THE STROKE

'Concentration is the ability to think about absolutely nothing when it is absolutely necessary.'

Ray Knight

When asked why he took so long over some of his putts, Jack Nicklaus said he was trying to empty his mind of all thoughts – to think of nothing at all.

Any thoughts during a shot are a distraction. They lead to uncertainty or even confusion. I would say that any thinking during the putting stroke is potentially harmful, as it shifts our focus from sinking the putt to controlling the strike of the ball.

In my previous books I explained that the key thought before we play a shot is the desired final resting place of the ball. Having selected our target, we should lock it in, and get on with playing the shot, without any intrusive or negative thoughts. On the putting green we can see the target – it is the hole – so we have less need to use our imagination. The challenge arises when our minds begin to distract us from this target.

There was a movie made back in the 1940s called *The Paleface*, which starred Bob Hope as a Harvard-educated dentist, Painless Potter, who goes to make his fortune in the Wild West. Potter is an innocent among the hard-living cowboys and criminals, but he tries to fit in by dressing as a cowboy and acting tough. One day in the saloon he gets into a disagreement with a gunslinger who challenges him to a duel outside in the street. Though dressed as a cowboy, Potter has never been in any kind of fight, let alone fired a gun. But the locals don't know this; they think he is the real deal, and as he slowly and nervously walks to the door, he receives well-intentioned advice from others in the bar.

The first piece of advice is, 'He draws from the left, so lean to the right.' Taking this advice, Potter starts to repeat it to himself like a mantra. No sooner has he done so than a second person tells him conspiratorially, 'There's a wind from the east, so aim to the left.' He takes this on board and again starts to repeat it, but with the first bit of advice too. As he gets to the door, a final person tells him, 'He crouches when he shoots, so stand on your toes.' Nodding his head as he hears this, the humble dentist is now trying to remember and combine all three bits of advice. The scene is very funny because in this absurd situation we see a man trying desperately to process some very complicated advice – when he's already completely out of his depth.

Like Painless Potter's, many golfers' minds chatter away as they stand over the ball, with thoughts, tips, advice and instruction – all well-intentioned but totally disruptive. How often do we think, 'The putt is downhill so don't hit it too hard,' or, 'The putter face looks a little shut so open it a fraction,' or, 'This green looks slow compared to the last one,' or 'Be sure to play the putt more off the toe of the club,' or some other instruction as we prepare to make our stroke?

We need to be able to still our minds over the putt. As Sam Snead answered with a smile when asked what he thought about when he was playing his best golf, we should think about 'Nothing at all'. Unfortunately, a 'silent mind' is not our natural state, so we need to develop our ability to achieve it. This can be done by taking time to sit quietly and, difficult as it may sound, just think of nothing at all. Try it. We may find random thoughts creeping in; the secret is to let go of every thought, positive or negative.

A useful exercise is to take the time, every day, to sit in a state of complete physical and mental stillness and think of nothing for thirty seconds. That's all: thirty seconds. Sounds easy, doesn't it? I'm sure it sounds odd too, but it serves a very useful purpose.

When we try this for the first time random thoughts about a variety of subjects from our subconscious will invade our conscious minds. We have these thoughts throughout the day, but normally we don't pay too much attention to them as we are engaged in another activity. It is only when there is no physical activity to distract us that we pay attention to such thoughts and give them previously undue meaning or value. In the process, we enter the opposite state of mind from that which we desire to work, play or create at our best. **Our aim should be to silence our minds of all thought.**

On the putting green we only need to still our thoughts when we make the stroke: maybe two seconds at the most. This is why the discipline of regularly doing it at home for thirty seconds at a time will put us in a better position to do so over a putt.

For all the acknowledgement of the importance of the mental game, very few golfers make it a part of their daily practice routine. Many players suffer from a false assumption that mental toughness rather than mental calm is what gets the job done. **What we practise we improve**, so if we make a habit of emptying our mind over the putt, it will allow our stroke to be more natural and less consciously influenced.

We are all aware of the 'pushed' putt that goes to the right and the equally undesirable 'pulled' putt that goes left. We know these putts as soon as we hit them, and quickly say, 'I pushed it,' or, 'I pulled it.' *We* did it. Somewhere between taking the club head back and returning it to the ball we changed the position of the putter head, or changed the path of our putter, from in to out or vice versa. This happens because we are still *thinking* about making perfect contact during the shot, rather than just letting it happen – as it would if we simply let go and surrendered to our instinct. By this point, the mechanical side of our stroke should have been set (that's the **ready** part), we are in position over the putt (the **steady** stage), and all that's left is to trust ourselves (that's the **go** – pure, unthinking action).

Allowing thoughts to enter our minds during the putt may seem like a small and subtle slip, but it will have a marked effect on our stroke. Though the misaligned contact with the ball may feel beyond our control, it is our own mental process that is creating the problem. We may be: not trusting our stroke and becoming too self-aware; or thinking about the stroke during the stroke; or trying too hard to be perfect. The solution is to **practise the outcome that we want to produce**. It is not, and never has been, enough to understand the theory alone.

I accept that as we get older there are many things that are and will remain beyond our abilities, due either to the degree of technical skill and execution they require, or to our diminishing suppleness and strength, but putting is not one of these things. We are all equal on the putting green, and, as we know, **perfect putting it is not about perfect technique: it is about finding our own perfection**, a level of trust that frees us up to be our best. I sincerely believe that stilling our minds over every shot makes a huge difference in helping us 'get out of our own way'. I recommend the following exercise.

DOWN THE LINE ▶

1. On the practice green, lay a piece of string on the ground, pulling it tight between two tees about thirty-six inches apart.

2. Put the middle of your putter head on the middle of the string, and watch your stroke as you make a series of practice swings.

3. Pay attention to the centre of your club head. Does the string remain in the middle of the club head at the impact point Often you will discover that you have an 'in-to-out' or 'out-to-in' path – and that's fine. What you need to ensure sure is that the club is not a little open or closed at the impact point.

4. Swing the club head consciously, striving to keep the middle of the club head over the string at the impact point.

5. Notice how this feels, continue to do it until you are consistently keeping the middle of the club head squarely over the string at impact. It does not matter if to accomplish this you have to change your stance, use a more wristy action, or feel as though you are putting from 'out to in', or 'in to out'.

6. Now continue this stroke with your eyes shut, every so often opening them to see if you are still square and in the middle through impact. Pay attention to the feeling of this stroke! This is what your stroke should always feel like.

The reason I like this exercise is that it builds the inner feeling of 'right action' necessary to keep the putter square through impact. When we have that feeling and learn to trust it, it becomes easier to still our mind over the stroke, as we will know by feeling that it is right.

27

THE UNAWARE PLAYER

'When a putter is waiting his turn to hole out
a putt of one or two feet in length, on which
the match hangs at the last hole, it is of vital
importance that he think of nothing. At this
supreme moment he ought to fill his mind
with vacancy. He must not even allow
himself the consolation of religion.'

Sir Walter Simpson, *The Art of Golf*

When I was a little boy my father, the local doctor, would on occasion have to give me an injection. Normally this would happen in the kitchen at home, and, though I was very young, I clearly remember the routine. When an injection was coming, my father would roll up my sleeve, rub some antiseptic on my skin, look idly out of the window, pause, and then exclaim, 'Gosh, look at that!' You can probably figure out the rest. Before I could finish saying, 'Ow!,' the painful task was complete. The distraction not only dispelled my concern over the injection, it also seemed to lessen the pain I had been anticipating.

Important putts bring with them added pressure, as they affect our chances of winning the game. At these times staring at our putt for a few minutes, reassessing the break, trying to work out a subtle nuance of the green or worrying about leaving the ball short (or long) are not helpful activities. So why do it? It is human nature to try to solve problems, and getting a ball into the hole from six feet to win a match is a problem of sorts. But few people like problems in high pressure situations – they stress us out, wear us down, exhaust us, and ultimately come to dominate our thoughts.

Over critical putts I find it helpful to mark the ball, take a look at the line, pick my spot, and then think about something else. Usually I take a look around at my surroundings, or sometimes I simply think of nothing at all. I don't speculate on missing the putt; in fact the last thing I think about is the putt! Over-thinking important putts breaks the routine. On pressure shots, many players over-analyse, spending longer than normal reading them. But the more we dwell on an important putt, the more pressure and uncertainty we unintentionally create.

Uncertainty can be fatal on the green, as it introduces tension into the stroke. Contrast days when we putt badly with the days when we putt superbly. Which days are easy, and which are frustrating and stressful? When we putt badly we get irritated, lose confidence and become plagued by self-doubt. We start expecting to miss the putt; we lose our feel; our distance-control deserts us. The days we remember vividly are those magical days when we putted superbly. There was no self-doubt; we were confident and relaxed; we expected to sink every putt – because the hole seemed as big as a bucket!

The main difference between these two scenarios is perception. **When we putt badly we perceive putts as difficult and ourselves as 'bad' putters; this makes us lose confidence, which is reinforced when we continue to play badly. Self-doubt inspires a self-fulfilling cycle of performance decline.** When we perceive putts as being easy or makeable, we relax and allow ourselves to make a positive stroke, less affected by unhelpful thoughts and emotions. As the putts drop, shave the hole or stop dead, this reinforces our self-confidence, our reading of the green, our stroke – our thoughts and emotions are then positive and helpful.

Let's go back to that kitchen in Glasgow back in the early 1960s, with my father administering the injection. His exclamation of, 'Gosh, look at that!', gazing out of the window as though he had just seen Ben Hogan walking up our garden path, was not something I imagine he did with any of his patients in the surgery. But he did it with me because he knew if he distracted my attention from the main object of my concern, I would momentarily relax and the experience would be less disagreeable. As I got older, an injection became less of a big deal. I learnt about my older sisters' 'injections for sweets' scheme, and the 'Gosh, look at that!' routine was no longer needed.

We too should learn to distract ourselves, or at least to become oblivious to pressure. This can be achieved through the techniques I have outlined in this book. It is much easier if we train ourselves to avoid feelings of anxiety.

The 'secret', such as it is, is to foster the habit of detaching ourselves from the outcome of the putt. I know this sounds difficult, especially when the putt is for a significant win or a course record, but if we can remove the emotional value from the putt and look at it dispassionately, in the isolation of pure logic, we will realise our situation boils down to these four basic truths:

1. We want to make the best putt we can. *We can only do this if we are mentally and technically prepared.*
2. Once we have played the stroke, the ball is either going to go in or it is not. *Worrying about missing the putt is pointless, and to do so adds tension.*
3. We know from statistical probability – our record-keeping – what the chances of the ball dropping are. *If we don't practise, that probability is not going to improve.*

4. We want to be in the best physical and mental state to take the putt.

The current putt is the only putt there is. The past is irrelevant. The future does not exist. We are, and must be, in the moment. The more we practise uncluttering our minds, removing unhelpful thoughts or anxieties, and the less we engage in negative self-talk, replacing it with positive encouragement, the closer we will come to freeing ourselves from the mental garbage (negative thoughts, despair, lack of confidence, anxiety, reliving poor past shots) that inhibits peak performance. We don't need negativity; we don't deserve it. So just dump it! If we can free ourselves from the mental pressures which afflict us on the green, we will make becoming the best putters we can be a reality.

Of course I understand the importance of winning, and that winning matters. Moreover, to say, 'Just relax and take it easy,' makes no sense unless we have a strategy for shutting out the emotional overloading that comes with pressure. Ultimately this means mastering a trick: the expectation that the shot *will* be made – a mind-set in which we putt like we never miss. In the final analysis, for all the words written about putting, it comes down to a stroke we trust and a strong mental game. Our beliefs at a subconscious level influence our actions at a conscious level. When we get in a car to drive somewhere we don't keep thinking about the destination to remind ourselves where we are going. We know – and then go.

If we believe we can improve and are willing to do what it takes to do so, we will. If we believe we are good putters, then, at a subconscious level, we will find evidence to validate that belief. We will forget the bad play and focus on the good.

THE RYDER CUP 2012

The 2012 Ryder Cup at Medinah Country Club in Illinois will be remembered as one of *the* classic encounters of the contest. For the first day and a half the Europeans were being roundly beaten. Their excuse was an honest and simple admission that they were being outplayed: the Americans were sinking putts, while they weren't. At the highest level, the game comes down to those critical inches on the green.

By lunchtime on the second day the US team led the Europeans 8–4. In the afternoon four-balls, the European team lost the first two matches. Now with a 10–4 lead, it was looking like a runaway win for the Americans. In the third match, Europe's Luke Donald and Sergio García built up a strong lead, going four up after nine, only to see Steve Stricker and Tiger Woods stage a charge and come back to one down with two holes to play. At the par-three seventeenth, Donald played one of the shots of his career when he put his ball inside Woods', itself only three feet from the hole. Europe hung on and won their match on the eighteenth, making the score 10–5.

The final match on the course featured Ian Poulter and Rory McIlroy against Zack Johnson and Jason Dufner. After twelve holes the US pairing were two up, with Europe needing to win the match for there to be even the remotest chance of them retaining the Ryder Cup the next day. McIlroy won the thirteenth with a birdie two, and this shifted the momentum in the match. What happened next is well known, but it was in my opinion the greatest putting display under pressure that I have ever witnessed. Poulter went on to make five clutch birdies over the next five holes, all the more impressive as the US team also birdied two of them. He demonstrated a combination of concentrated focus and self-belief over every shot he played, but on the greens in particular he was magical. The resulting win kept Europe in the contest.

As an example of the power of setting ambitious goals and a phenomenal drive to succeed, I can think of no one better than Poulter. Even as a young teenage assistant pro he had set his sights on playing on the USPGA tour. He had a great work ethic and knew what he had to do to make his dreams a reality. Lee Scarbrow, the head pro at Leighton Buzzard golf club and Poulter's coach and boss for over five years, said of him, 'Ian was so focused on the end goal, of being a top-class golf pro. He believed in what he wanted to do and understood what he needed to do to get there. He was always going to be a European tour winner and a Ryder Cup player. He never spoke to me about if, just when.'

In my work over the past twenty years, studying and speaking about success and peak performance, I have found that, without exception, the high achievers in sport and life exhibit three things:

1. a clearly defined goal,
2. a considered but flexible plan to realise their goal,
3. an unshakeable belief that it can be done.

Lee Scarbrow said in an article in a UK golf magazine in 2012, 'It was Ian's mentality rather than his technique that got him where he is today.' Of Poulter's putting he said, 'Ian's a great putter under pressure because he is so focused and believes in the roll he puts on a golf ball. He has a great imagination and ability to see the line of the putts. The more pressure he's under, the more focused he becomes and the better he plays. That plays into his hands at Ryder Cups when the pressure is so intense.'

After the Europeans went on, in dramatic fashion, to win the singles 8½–3½ the following day, and seal a famous and improbable victory, I heard two quotes from interviews by the eighteenth green that captured the essence of high-level, high-pressure performance.

Ian Poulter, when asked to explain where his game-changing performance had come from, hesitated for a second, before saying simply, 'It came from within.' That was his best way of articulating something which eludes description.

However, the quote I found most meaningful came from Martin Kaymer. With the score at 13–13, Kaymer had arrived on the eighteenth green needing a six-foot putt to win his match and retain the Ryder Cup for Europe. It was a putt not for personal glory but for his team, for his captain, José María Olazábal, and for golf fans across Europe. It was a putt of immense magnitude and, under the circumstances, as tough a six-foot putt as you could ever imagine.

Kaymer told his interviewer that when he walked up to the putt he said to himself, 'Just make it; don't think about anything else. Just make it.' He didn't contemplate missing it; he didn't entertain any thought other than, 'Just make it.' Brilliant!

Good luck and from now on putt like you never miss.

ABOUT THE AUTHOR

Robin Sieger is a bestselling author, motivational speaker and performance coach, with offices in the UK and the USA.

At the age of 29 he was diagnosed with cancer and it was this life changing experience that made him determine to re-examine his notion of success. He now works as a keynote business speaker and performance coach all over the world and his humour and ability to connect emotionally with audiences has made him the first-choice speaker at major conferences for some of the world's most successful companies, including HP, GM, HSBC, IBM, Coca-Cola, Ford, Nokia and Microsoft, where he received the highest ranking of any external speaker.

He is the author of six other books including the international bestseller *Natural Born Winners*, which is sold in over 80 countries worldwide, and *Silent Mind Golf*. He is also the visiting mental game coach at the Concession Golf Club Florida and holds the world record for the coldest round of golf ever played, 18 holes at −26°C in Fairbanks, Alaska on 22 December 2001.

For more information on mental game golf instruction offered by Robin Sieger, please visit www.siegergolf.com or send an e-mail to info@siegergolf.com.

You may write directly to robin@siegergolf.com.

He travels internationally delivering keynote motivational presentations to organisations, institutions and companies worldwide. His company, Sieger International, offers a wide range of seminars and educational programmes on peak performance and success to both the public and private sector.

For more information about how to book Robin or Sieger International Trainers please visit www.siegergolf.com.

To enquire about golf instruction for corporate golf outings, private lessons or a keynote talk at a business event, please contact:

In the UK
0845 2305400

In the USA
941 313 6859

David Leadbetter has long been regarded as one of the world's premier golf instructors for players at all levels. He has coached six world number one golfers who have won over a dozen majors between them. The author of seven acclaimed instructional books on golf, he has also produced numerous videos about the game, and writes for the world's leading golfing publications, including *Golf Digest*.